Men @ Work

HOW MEN CAN RENEW THEIR COMMITMENTS TO GOD, TO FAMILY, AND TO THEMSELVES

Dr. I.V. Hilliard

Harrison House
Tulsa, Oklahoma

16 15 14 13   10 9 8 7 6 5 4 3 2

Men @ Work:
How Men Can Renew Their Commitments to God, to Family, and to Themselves
ISBN 13: 978-1-57794-973-2
ISBN 10: 1-57794-973-0
Copyright © 2008 by Light Publications
P.O. Box 670167
Houston, TX 77267 www.newlight.org

Published by Harrison House, Inc.
P.O. Box 35035
Tulsa, Oklahoma 74153 www.harrisonhouse.com

Dedication

I would like to dedicate this book to my father, Theodore Hilliard, Sr., who taught me how to respect manhood. Even though he only received an elementary school education, he was wise in his own right. My father taught me to always have an open heart to learn and, through example, he taught me the value of a strong work ethic. He knew that as I journeyed through life, I would have opportunities to meet and gain wisdom and insight from other great men. He taught me how to value their time and treasure the learning moment. From that foundational lesson I have grown, and through my own first hand experiences I now teach my congregation that, *"We are all the sum total of what others invest in our lives, that we choose to incorporate into our lives."*

I am forever grateful to my father for making the initial investment, the down payment in my life, that paved the way for others to make valuable installments that have caused me to be the man I am today.

Acknowledgements

I give honor and thanks to God for His Holy Spirit who is within me, teaching me, and guiding me through awesome projects like this, *Men @ Work.*

Thanks to my beautiful wife, Lady Bridget, for your continued support and dedication throughout the years. My life would not be as fulfilled and rewarding without you at my side. Your encouragement and help with this project is invaluable. This important work that helps establish the manhood legacy of my life would not have been completed without your assistance and participation.

Thanks to my children, Terry and Tina Egans, Jeff and Irishea Lewis, and Preashea Hilliard. I am so godly proud of you. Each one of you are following the course that God and your parents have developed for you. I am excited about what God is doing in your life and I am in continued expectation of what He is going to do. The best is yet to come.

To my grandchildren, Ira-Emanuel, Briona, Ivan, and Jonathan—Big Daddy loves you.

To the wonderful congregation of New Light Church World Outreach and Worship Centers in Houston (North, South, and East), Beaumont, and Austin, Texas. A church is only as great as the members who are a part of it. That is why I am proud to say, New Light—you are a great church—you are truly *"The Church Like No Other!"* Thank you for being committed to the vision. I've told you before, but please let me say it again, thank you for allowing me to be your pastor and always know that your pastor loves you.

And special thanks to my first born daughter Mrs. Tina Hilliard-Egans who spear-headed this project from start to finish, bringing to fruition this labor of love so that others could be blessed by the wisdom captured in these pages.

Finally, to Mrs. Filecha Lucas, a special editor, for your assistance on this project that exposes my heart on manhood matters.

Table of Contents

Introduction

We all admire men who have worked hard to achieve great levels of success in their lives. We have seen great men work and develop themselves intellectually and help advance this world's technology. We have seen great men work and develop themselves in the political arena and make great gains in the civil causes, we have seen great men work and foster good relationships with loved ones and build a great family life, but the most noble of all of these men are those who choose to work and develop their character, for in developing their character, all areas of their lives will be the better. *Men @ Work,* highlights the principles that are needed to work on your ministry, your money, your marriage, repairing mistakes you have made in the past and so much more. This book is a tool you can use to learn valuable principles that will help you achieve the success you admire in others. Once you understand these principles, you must put them into practice for them to positively affect your character and make a difference in your life. There is no substitute for perseverance because the only way you'll see results is if you don't quit. You have to stay with any life-changing process to get the promised results!

I want to share a story that I believe will help you see this.

I'm from Houston, but the best chocolate cake I've ever had was in Palm Springs, California. Some time ago I preached at a church in Fontana, California. One night while we were having dinner there the pastor told me that we were only 35 minutes from Palm Springs. Thirty-five minutes from the place where I love to go. And I go there for one reason: this cake.

So the pastor said, "We'll take you tomorrow. We can have lunch there." I said, "Okay, fine." I knew it was going to take more than 35 minutes to get there because I'd looked at the map. But it didn't matter. I was willing to pay the price.

It took us about an hour to get there. No problem. I was going to get some of that cake. I didn't even like to eat at the place because the rest of the food wasn't that great. So we had lunch at another restaurant and then we headed over to this place for dessert. I knew how they served that chocolate cake. They cut it in really big pieces, put ice cream on it, and baptized it in hot chocolate sauce. It was the best cake I'd eaten in my entire life. I'd eaten cake all over the world, and I'd never found anything like this cake.

We pulled up in front of the restaurant where they serve this cake and there was a sign hanging on the door: Closed. I jumped out of the car, ran to the door, and started banging on it. Bam! Bam! Bam! A little girl came to the door. She looked scared. Here was this 235-pound, 6-foot-1 black man wearing a hat and dark sunglasses banging on the door. I knew I frightened her, so I said, "Go get the manager." A man came to the door. I said, "I have come too far. I want a chocolate cake. I will not be denied." He opened the door and said, "Come right on in!" I did. I bought an entire cake and took it with me.

That man at the restaurant looked in my eyes and saw that I wasn't going to leave without a cake. He understood. The sign on the door said Closed, but he knew. I found out he was the new owner. He had just bought the place. I told him, "Change anything you want to in here, but don't change the cake." He said, "The lady who's been making the cakes for 10 years is still here. She makes them fresh every day." I said, "All right. Don't change my cake!"

I bought the cake and took it back to my hotel room. Every day I cut a little slice and ate it. The pastor tasted it and it blew him away. He almost wanted to take my cake. I told him, "You're right down the street. You can go get cake any time you want to. I'm taking my cake back to Texas!"

Some time after I got home, my wife called that restaurant and ordered two more cakes. Recently I walked into the office and the staff had sliced up the cakes and were feeding everybody. Everyone was enjoying what I had enjoyed, all because I would not be denied.

The point of this story is, most men quit too easily. They let the least sign of disappointment discourage them from pursuing their dream when what they want is within their reach, if they'll be bold enough not to be denied.

When you read statements and principles in this book that speak to areas in your life where you know you need to change and you want to change, go after that change and don't be denied. To achieve success, that's the way you have to be. What you will end up with is a whole lot more valuable than chocolate cake. Both you and your family can be blessed if you will just decide that you will not be denied.

A Man and His Maker

In the first chapter of this book we're going to establish a scriptural relationship between a man and His Creator. Man needs to know his purpose—his reason for being. My goal is that every man who reads this book will understand this foundational truth of his created purpose and then learn how to stay in that purpose consistently by obeying God.

Let's begin by looking at several verses in Genesis chapter 1.

Genesis 1:26–28

26 And God said, Let us make man in our image, after our likeness: and let them have dominion over the fish of the sea, and over the fowl of the air, and over the cattle, and over all the earth, and over every creeping thing that creepeth upon the earth.

27 God created man in his own image, in the image of God created he him; male and female created he them.

28 And God blessed them, and God said unto them, Be fruitful, and multiply, and replenish the earth, and subdue it: and have dominion over the fish of the sea, and over the

fowl of the air, and over every living thing that moveth upon the earth.

This scripture clearly declares that God is our Creator. And that establishes His right to direct our lives. It is the exclusive right of the maker of a thing to determine why the thing was made and how the thing made best functions. So since God is our Maker, God alone has the right to tell us why we were made.

When I look for purpose—and purpose is the key to fulfillment—I don't look outside of this creative spectrum. The Bible clearly says that we were created in the image of God. God spoke some things over man. And to the degree that we understand what God created us to do—why He made us—and walk in that purpose, we will experience fulfillment in life.

A thing's purpose is the reason for its existence. Only when a thing carries out its created purpose will fulfillment take place. For instance, if you're seated in a chair as you read this, that chair is designed to hold your weight in a seated position. If you stood in the chair, you would be abusing its purpose. But because you are seated in the chair, it is fulfilling its purpose.

So it is when I find out what God wants me to do—why I was created—to the degree that I do what God created me to do, I experience fulfillment. Apart from that, I spend my life chasing fulfillment decoys—pursuits that look like they will be fulfilling, but aren't.

The Key to Fulfillment

When God told man to subdue the earth and have dominion, He was saying He wanted to work with man. So the key to man's fulfillment is his relationship with the Lord. In order for man to have this relationship, he must respect God's rights over his life.

Now man has been created with a desire and a need to have a god. Man has to have a god. That god might be sports, or his hobby, or something else that he can give himself wholly to. He may be driving his god, or his god may be in his pocket, but he's got a god because he has to have one. Man has been designed like that. If he does not give his allegiance to His Creator, he'll find something else to worship. Romans 10:3 says, "For they being ignorant of God's righteousness, and going about to establish their own righteousness, have not submitted themselves unto the righteousness of God."

We have a void in our lives that must be filled, and in an attempt to fill that void, we go on a search. God created us this way because it was His intent that the search would lead us to Him.

That's why people in some countries have a god for everything. They bow down to rocks and cows, because God has engineered us in such a way that we need to give obedience to something greater than ourselves. We have to depend on something far greater than we are. So we're in a search for God.

The Scriptures tell us that a man discovers this lordship factor when he understands that he was made by the God of the universe, Who has an awesome plan for his life. This plan includes his accepting Jesus as Savior and Lord.

Lordship is God's design for man's relationship with Him. In other words, God doesn't want to be your partner; He wants to be your Lord. He's not your running buddy. He's your Lord.

So I have to see that since God is my Creator, He alone has the right to tell me what to do. And until somebody else makes a world and writes a Bible, I'm going to go with the One Who did those things.

In Romans chapter 10, we find a simple formula for establishing a relationship with God.

ROMANS 10:9

9 That if thou shalt confess with thy mouth the Lord Jesus, and shalt believe in thine heart that God hath raised him from the dead, thou shalt be saved.

Man could not save himself. Adam messed up. God gave man some specific instructions in the garden, and man did not follow those instructions.

Many people ask, "Why did God put the tree with that forbidden fruit in the Garden? Was God trying to trick man? If God hadn't put that tree there, man would never have had an opportunity to mess up." The reason God put that tree in the Garden is quite simple. God created man in His image. He created him innocent, but He did not create him spiritually mature. In order to mature spiritually, you have to have an object of obedience. So God put the tree in the Garden to give man the opportunity to obey Him. And as man would regularly obey Him, he would grow in trust and allegiance to God.

So the tree wasn't there to trick man; it was there to help him mature. But man violated God's plan, ate from the tree, and did what God told him not to do. The Bible says that God told man that the day he ate of that fruit he would die (Gen. 2:17). When man ate, he did not die physically; he died spiritually.

Adam's disobedience caused sin to get into the bloodline of mankind. Now, every man is born in sin and has a sin debt that must be paid. So God sent Jesus, Who was without sin, to pay the price for man's sin. The Bible says that when I accept that Jesus paid the price for my sins and that He was raised from the dead—which validated all He said He was—I am saved. I am born again.

To understand the new birth, you have to understand that God created us as three-part beings: body, soul, and spirit. We're spirit beings living inside physical bodies, and we possess a soul. When I'm born again, my hands don't change. Maybe you grew up in a church where people said after they were born again, "I looked at my hands and my hands looked new." That's good preaching, but the reality is, your hand size doesn't change when you're born again. Your foot size doesn't change. When the Bible tells you in Second Corinthians 5:17 that you're a new creature, you're not physically new. You've become spiritually new, spiritually alive to God. That's what being born again means. But once you're spiritually alive to God, you need to know why you're here. You need to know your purpose.

God's original plan for man was for man to actively partic-ipate with Him in having dominion on the earth and that plan hasn't changed. When I am born again, God's original plan is still, in principle, the one I'm supposed to follow. I've been created in this earth to participate with God in dominion—to participate with Him in ruling the earth.

We see something about this in Ephesians chapter 2.

Ephesians 2:10

10 For we are his workmanship, created in Christ Jesus unto good works, which God hath before ordained that we should walk in them.

The Amplified Bible says it this way:

Ephesians 2:10

10 For we are God's [own] handiwork (His workmanship), recreated in Christ Jesus, [born anew] that we may do those good works which God predestined (planned beforehand) for us, (taking paths which He prepared ahead of time) that we should walk in them—living the good life which He prearranged and made ready for us to live.

So I understand clearly from the Word of God that He created me to be involved with Him and work with Him in His program for the earth. There are some things God cannot do in the earth without man's participation and permission. Many people don't understand that. Many of us who grew up in church were told that God could do anything He wanted to do. That's not necessarily the case.

That's not to slight the sovereignty of God. It's just that God has an order He set up, and He must respect that order. Part of that order is, the only way to operate in authority in the earth is through a body. Look in Ezekiel chapter 22.

Ezekiel 22:30–31

30 And I sought for a man among them, that should make up the hedge, and stand in the gap before me for the land, that I should not destroy it: but I found none.

31 Therefore have I poured out mine indignation upon them; I have consumed them with the fire of my wrath: their

own way have I recompensed upon their heads, saith the Lord God.

Because of sin, God's wrath should come upon the earth. God is saying, "I don't want my wrath to come. If I can find somebody in the earth who will stand in the gap and intercede and petition me not to destroy the earth, then I have a justifiable right to withhold My wrath." But God said that since He couldn't find anyone, His wrath has to run its course.

I see in this passage that God can't do just anything He wants to do, because if He could He wouldn't need to look for a man. He'd just haul off and do what He wants to do, but He set a certain order in the earth.

How to Discover Your Purpose

God has a master plan for the earth. When you understand that, you'll know that you're not here by accident. But how do you discover your purpose? How do you find out what God has you here to do?

First, *you discover your purpose by what God has specifically told you.* And if God hasn't told you anything, don't lie and make something up.

Second, *you discover your purpose by what God is doing in your family.* For instance, we see in the Bible that both Samuel and John the Baptist had already been dedicated to the Lord before they were born. Their roles in life were already established by their families. So John couldn't come on the scene and say, "I'm going to be a chariot mechanic," because it had already been destined that he was to be a prophet.

Now, John the Baptist wasn't going to be any less fulfilled as a prophet than as a chariot mechanic, because a man's fulfillment is tied to his purpose. As long as he lived out his purpose, no matter what that purpose was, he would walk in a level of fulfillment.

What if God hasn't said anything to you, and you don't know whether He is doing anything in your family? You might be the only one in your family who is saved.

In Acts chapter 16 we get scriptural insight into how we can discover our individual purpose. Once we discover our purpose, we're on our way to fulfilling it.

Acts 16:9–10

9 And a vision appeared to Paul in the night; There stood a man of Macedonia, and prayed him, saying, Come over into Macedonia, and help us.

10 And after he had seen the vision, immediately we endeavoured to go into Macedonia, assuredly gathering that the Lord had called us for to preach the gospel unto them.

I want you to see this, because this is so important. Only Paul saw the vision. He shared the vision with those who had committed to help him, *and they received that as their calling too.* So their calling and purpose were defined by the vision of the man of God under whom God had set them.

You see, I don't have to search blindly to find my purpose. I just need to get connected to a man with a vision. And until God tells me something different, I just lock into that, because my purpose will be defined by the vision I'm set under.

Remember, the plan of God is preordained. That means that when you were a little boy and God was taking you through various situations, He was getting you ready for the vision of the man of God whom you're set under. So where you are at is not a mistake, no matter where you come from. God may have brought you from another city or another state to sit under a certain man of God. The bottom line is, God has been in this all the while. Even when you didn't know it, He had people along the way pushing you back on track. His plan for you was preordained, because your purpose is tied to some man's vision. When you hook up with that vision, you're on your way to fulfillment.

The Importance of Obeying God

Every man must value and understand the importance of obeying God. I cannot stay on the track of His purpose for me and find fulfillment unless I obey Him.

Obedience is willing submission to the orders and instructions of one in authority[1]. To obey God means to obey His statutes or commandments. To follow God's purpose for my life, I've got to obey Him. I have to be willing to do what He says to do.

All of us are going to live by some standard. We're going to surrender our thinking to something. When we make Jesus Lord, we say that from now on we will do what He tells us to do.

That's why men make good Christians. Once we make up our mind to do something, we can do it. That's also why men make good warriors. When we have focus and purpose, we can carry out an assignment even to the death. God designed us that way. But maturity comes when a man decides to obey God.

I can be born again and then live in rebellion against God's ways and not be fulfilled, because I keep getting off track. But fulfillment comes when I understand what God wants and I choose to obey Him. Look at these verses in Isaiah chapter 1.

Isaiah 1:19–20

19 If ye be willing and obedient, ye shall eat the good of the land:

20 But if ye refuse and rebel, ye shall be devoured with the sword: for the mouth of the LORD hath spoken it.

When the Bible talks about being devoured by the sword, that means the weapon of your enemy will overcome you. I must understand that if I want to be free from the weapons of my enemy, I must walk in obedience. There is no substitute for obedience. Every act of disobedience to the known will of God is a calculated act of rebellion that calls into question the condition of my heart. In other words, when I know what God wants me to do and I choose to do something else, I am rebelling against Him. That raises the question of whether my heart is right toward Him.

It's really not hard to obey God, because we've been designed to obey Him. It's harder for me to walk in disobedience. Proverbs 13:15 says the way of transgressors is hard. Science has even found that when a person lies, his body functions abnormally. That's why a polygraph test works, because God didn't design us to lie. We were designed to tell the truth. We function better when we walk in truth. It takes a lot of energy to lie, because we have to remember the lie, and then we have to connect other issues together to make the lie sound right. We need to put away lying (Eph. 4:25).

Making Tough Choices

We will stay on course with God and continue to grow spiritually to the degree that we are willing to consistently make tough choices in agreement with God's purpose and plan for our life. God said, "If ye be willing and obedient, ye shall eat the good of the land" (Isa. 1:19). We all want the good of the land. To get that, we need to act like men and obey God. He designed us and created us to walk in obedience to Him.

Look at Joshua chapter 1. Here God tells Joshua what he needs to do for his life to go to the next level.

Joshua 1:8

8 This book of the law shall not depart out of thy mouth; but thou shalt meditate therein day and night, that thou mayest observe to do [or obey] according to all that is written therein: for then thou shalt make thy way prosperous, and then thou shalt have good success.

If we're designed to obey God and our obedience will bring us God's best, then why does it seem difficult for us to obey?

First, it can seem hard for us to obey God because we may have some unsurrendered areas in our lives that clash with the Word of God. In other words, we've made Him Lord over some areas but we haven't given Him the right to tell us what to do in other areas. In those other areas, we're telling Him, "Well now, hold on. I don't want to do that."

It might be that in your sex life you're telling God, "I know what You said about adultery and fornication, but right now I have needs. I have feelings. I have hormones."

Second, it can seem difficult for us to obey God when our obedience puts us at odds with people we believe we need acceptance and approval from. Many times, approval and acceptance from other folks means more to us than obeying God. And to the degree that we believe we need acceptance and approval from others, we will compromise obedience to God to get that acceptance.

Young men need to learn this lesson early, because most of the trouble guys get into, somebody else gets them into it. Someone exploits their innocence. You desire acceptance from someone you are looking up to, and you let them steer you off track. You have to settle in your heart that you need acceptance from God and God alone.

So I have to develop the attitude that if someone kicks me to the curb and doesn't want to be my friend because I refuse to go the way they want me to go to get their acceptance, so be it, because I'm going to be a long-distance runner. I'm going to be willing and obedient to do what God says to do, because I intend to eat the good of the land.

Third, it can seem hard to obey God because I may have a low tolerance for short-term discomfort. Many times, obeying God leads to some short-term discomfort. For example, let's talk about tithing. The tithe—the first tenth of my income—belongs to the Lord (see Malachi 3:7–12). When I start to tithe, initially it can be uncomfortable because I've been living off what I've been stealing from God. But short-term discomfort is okay if I'm a long-distance runner. If I'll stick with it, I'll outlast short-term discomfort.

Fourth, it can seem difficult to obey God when I see temporal success as proof that all is well. In other words, I say, "I'm doing all right. I have a good job and a good house. I don't have to do all that Christian stuff." The Bible says the psalmist was confused about that one day himself (see Psalm 73). He told God that it looked as though the wicked were flourishing. But he finally saw that the end of their life was destruction.

Fifth, it can seem difficult to obey God when I entertain postponement as an acceptable option. In other words, I say, "I'm going to get around to obeying God one of these days." That may pacify my mind, but it puts me in a state of disobedience and rebellion.

Sixth, it can seem difficult for me to obey God when I have no support group to encourage me in right living. That's why I need to be connected to a network of righteous men who are on their way to the same place I am, so that iron can sharpen iron, as Proverbs 27:17 says. In that network, we can keep each other on track and be accountable to each other. I need a network. I need the support of others.

How to Obey Consistently

So how do I obey God consistently? Here are four ways God taught me years ago. Number one, if I'm going to obey God consistently, gaining God's acceptance must be the most important thing in my life. Being accepted by Him is the only thing that matters. As long as I'm obeying God and I know I'm doing what He wants me to do, that's enough. I don't have to have you like me. The Bible says that when a man's ways please the Lord, He makes even the man's enemies be at peace with him (Prov. 16:7). So when I please God, I know that, even if you are my enemy, eventually you're not going to want to bother me.

Number two, obeying God consistently requires bold acts of obedience without complete understanding. In other words, I've got to be willing to trust that God knows what's best for me. So if He tells me to jump, I need to be ready to jump. God is not obligated to show me where He is leading me even though He knows. He gives me information on a need-to-know basis, and I must be satisfied with what He gives me.

I don't have to know the details of how everything is going to end up. I just have to know what step to take now, because after I take that step, then God is obligated to show me the next step. But He's not obligated to do that until I walk in the knowledge I already have.

Number three, if I'm going to consistently obey God, I cannot meditate on options for disobedience. I cannot consider how I can disobey and then recover from it. A minister I once talked to wanted to leave his wife. He was the pastor of a church, and he was talking about how many members he could lose and still make it.

I said, "Do you hear what you're saying? You're planning to disobey God! You think you're smart enough to make it." I told him the Bible teaches us to cast down imaginations and every high thing that exalts itself against the knowledge of God (2 Cor. 10:5). I need to do that because if I listen to the devil long enough, he will minimize the consequences of disobedience.

I was talking with some young men one day, and one of them said, "Doing time in jail isn't hard. I can do the time." I said, "You fool. Folks in jail are trying to get *out*of jail, and here you are out of jail bragging about what you can do when you get *into* jail."

Finally, to consistently obey God I must appropriate the measure of grace to obey under pressure. I've been designed to handle pressure and have dominion. God spoke that into my life, and whenever God speaks something, the thing that He speaks to immediately has the capacity, without instruction, to do what He told it to do. The bird needs no instructions on how to fly because God spoke that into it. The fish needs no swimming lessons, because God spoke how to swim into it. So when God made me in His image and likeness and told me to be fruitful and multiply, He engineered me to be more than what I look like right now.

The price for success is paid in two installments. The first installment is paid up front—in repentance and change. In other words, I've got to say that from now on I'm going to live a different way. I have to decide once and for all, "I'm going God's way." The second installment is paid through daily obedience. When I pay the price, I'm on track to fulfillment. And I will reach fulfillment when I commit to do what God wants me to do.

1) AM I GOING GODS WAY?
(Repentance / Change)

2) AM I walking in obedience to God's word
(Commitment & obedience)

2

A Man and
His Mountains

*Man that is born of a woman is of few days
and full of trouble.*
Job 14:1

The word *mountain* in this chapter symbolizes problems and troubles that we face in life. We all may not face the same kind of problems or trouble, but the Bible is clear that trouble is common to the human experience. You probably don't need a scripture on that. You know it already.

I can safely say that you are either facing a problem, or you are in the midst of a problem, or you're coming out of some problem. But the good thing about it is—and the Bible is so clear on this—Jesus came to give us life, and that more abun-dantly. In this chapter, I want you to get your head clear so you'll understand whose team you're on.

A lot of people think God is putting the problem on them, and that's not what the Scriptures say. Jesus said in John 10:10, "The thief cometh not, but for to steal, and to kill, and to destroy: I am come that they might have life, and that they might have it more abundantly."

Based on this scripture, I can clearly evaluate life's situations. If they are stealing, killing, and destroying, they aren't from God. That's simple. I need to make sure that I get my theology right so that I know when something is from God and when it isn't. Now when you're off course and not following God's ways, or you're willfully disobeying Him, there is the judgment factor. But when you're walking upright before God and doing the things you know He's told you to do, you know that any stealing, killing, or destroying that comes is not from Him.

The testimony of scripture reveals that there are many types of trouble. I think the Bible is really a book that talks about the trouble people have and how God gets them out of it. Job had trouble. Adam had trouble. Jehoshaphat had trouble. David had trouble. The widow of First Kings chapter 17 had trouble. The widow of Second Kings 4:1 had trouble. The Prodigal Son had trouble. Paul and Silas had trouble. Jesus had trouble. Peter had trouble. All of them had trouble.

The good part about this is, God didn't fool us. He never told us we wouldn't have problems. I think this clears the air for us so we understand what we're getting into when we choose to follow Jesus Christ. I've heard people present Christianity as insurance against trouble. Then when a person who is born again has trouble, he says, "I thought that because I'm saved, I wasn't supposed to go through that." No, somebody misled him. They didn't tell him the whole truth. The whole truth is that as long as we are in this world, we're going to have trouble whether we're saved or not. So don't tell me that old story, "I never had trouble before I was saved, and now I have a lot of trouble." No, you were having trouble before you got saved, because the Bible says man born of a woman is of few days and is full of trouble.

Psalm 34:19 says, "Many are the afflictions of the righteous: but the LORD delivereth him out of them all." This verse tells us the righteous will have troubles, but it also says that God will deliver us out of all of them. And there are many more scriptures that tell us God has committed to help us in trouble. That's good news! Trouble does not cancel the will of God to help us. When we go through trouble, that doesn't mean God has abandoned us. He's with us even in the midst of trouble.

So when I find myself in trouble, I'm not by myself. God is still committed to me, and He's equipped me to be an overcomer. I can see this in the Book of First John.

1 John 5:4
4 For whatsoever is born of God overcometh the world: and this is the victory that overcometh the world, even our faith.

According to this verse, God has equipped me to overcome, and I overcome by faith.

Our Ability to Reign Depends on Revelation

Our ability to reign in life depends on the revelation we have and the attitude we choose to adopt in the situations that we're in. In other words, depending on our attitude, the same situation can be what the Bible calls a light affliction, or it can be devastating.

I've been designed to overcome, and God says He'll deliver me out of all my troubles. To the degree I believe that and act on that, my attitude about trouble will change. I will see trouble differently, because I'll know, "I'm going to get through this. I'm coming out." Why? Because God said so. At the moment, I may not know how I'm going to come out of trouble, but I'll know I'm coming out.

So my attitude in the midst of trouble will be based on the revelation that I have of God's Word. What did God say about trouble? Remember: I'm born again now and I've made Him Lord, so what He says is most important. I couldn't care less about what somebody else says. That doesn't matter to me. I have God's Word that He'll deliver me out of all my troubles and that I will overcome.

Jesus said something about trouble in John chapter 16.

John 16:33
33 These things I have spoken unto you, that in me ye might have peace. In the world ye shall have tribulation: but be of good cheer; I have overcome the world.

Now look at how *The Amplified Bible* translates this verse:

John 16:33
33 I have told you these things, so that in Me you may have [perfect] peace and confidence. In the world you have tribulation and trials and distress and frustration; but be of good cheer [take courage; be confident, certain, undaunted]! For I have overcome the world. [I have deprived it of power to harm you and have conquered it for you.]

Jesus said that in Him you can have peace because even though the world is full of trouble, He has deprived it of power to harm you. To the degree that you believe that, you're going to act like it.

If you play football or basketball or some other sport, have you ever been behind in a game but you knew you were going to win? You knew you had the skill set, and you were going to win. The score may not have showed it at the moment, but you didn't throw in the towel. That's the attitude a man has to have about trouble. He has to believe, "I'm coming out of this." And to the degree that your family sees you walking in that attitude, they're going to be at peace.

We Must Prepare for Trouble

Since trouble is inescapable and avoiding trouble is impossible, then preparing for trouble is imperative. We have to get ready for the fight. Since the Bible says we're going to overcome by faith, then we need to be equipped on how to deal with trouble, because it's not the will of God for trouble to mess up our lives.

I call trouble and problems wake-up calls for our divine potential, because God will never let us get into trouble that we can't handle. You have to understand that. Look at this verse in First Corinthians chapter 10:

1 Corinthians 10:13
13 There hath no temptation taken you but such as is common to man....

First of all, you need to know that you're not the only one going through what you're going through. The devil likes to tell you, "You're the only one." You're not the only one, man.

You're not the only one who lost his job, or who ever had a drug problem, or whose wife is acting up. Now look at the rest of this verse.

1 Corinthians 10:13

13 ...but God is faithful, who will not suffer you to be tempted above that ye are able; but will with the temptation also make a way to escape, that ye may be able to bear it.

You see, whenever I go through trouble, I need to understand that God wouldn't even let me be in that situation if He hadn't equipped me to handle it, and in the end, I'm coming out on top. When the dust settles, I'm going to be standing. If you see me in a fight with a bear, you'd better help the bear, because that bear is going down.

The Bible says God will not let you get into a situation that you can't handle. That means if you are in trouble now, He already knows you are equipped to handle it, but you have to believe that. You have to believe that you can handle it because God's Word says you can. You have to trust His Word. The Word of God says He is faithful. He will never let you be in a situation that you can't handle, and He will always make a way for you to escape and bear the trouble. In other words, He guarantees your victory.

If I'm going to navigate through the trouble and overcome it, I need to know some things. Questions that we ask when facing troubled times can be answered from God's Word. I need to know why I am going through the trouble and what I need to do to get out of this trouble. If I don't deal with trouble right, trouble will bother my self-esteem—how I feel about myself. Scars left from past troubles deprive men of confidence.

First let's look at this verse in Proverbs chapter 26.

Proverbs 26:2

2 As the bird by wandering, as the swallow by flying, so the curse causeless shall not come.

This verse says there's a reason why things happen. I need to know why trouble came. There are four basic reasons why trouble comes into your life.

1. *Human error.* The Prodigal Son, Achan (Josh. 7:1), and Samson each made mistakes that caused trouble to come. Many times we make errors, ignorantly or intentionally. Sometimes we think we can do something we know is wrong and get away with it.

2. *Satanic attack.* That's what happened to Job. The Bible says that the devil was taking away from Job, so his situation was caused by Satan. Many times when Jesus would minister to people He would come against the evil spirit that was attacking them.

3. *The challenge of the times.* I am living in the world, so I am affected temporarily by what goes on around me. According to First Kings 17:7, the brook where Elijah was staying dried up not because he had not been praying, not because he was not where God wanted him to be, but because there had been no rain in the land. So Elijah had to suffer some discomfort because of the challenge of the times. There have been times when good, praying, tithing men have lost their jobs because there was downsizing in the industry in which they worked. But even in challenging times, I have the assurance that God will deliver me out of all my troubles.

4. *The call of God.* Because of the call of God on your life, you may have to wade through some trouble. David had no idea that he would wake up one morning and before the end of the day be faced with a giant. Paul and Silas didn't do anything wrong. They went where God told them to go, did what God told them to do, cast out a devil, and then found themselves whipped, beaten, and in jail. But it wasn't over.

I need to identify why the trouble I'm in came. If I caused it, I want to have the wisdom not to make that mistake any more. I need to learn that lesson, because a lesson not learned will always be repeated, and I don't want to go through that class again.

How to Get Out of Trouble

So how do I get out of trouble? Look again in First John chapter 5:

1 John 5:4
4 For whatsoever is born of God overcometh the world: and this is the victory that overcometh the world, even our faith.

My faith is going to get me out of trouble, but faith is a process. My getting out of trouble depends more on how I choose to face trouble than the magnitude of the trouble. Here's what I mean by that: The process of faith is the same whether I am believing for a sandwich or a whole loaf of bread. If I master the process at a low level, then it's no problem for me to do the same thing at a higher level with bigger results. If I learn how to handle small problems, I can use the same process to handle bigger problems. I already know, "Many are the afflictions of the righteous: but the LORD delivereth him out of them all" (Ps. 34:19), and I plan to be righteous. I plan to stay right with God. I'm holding on to the right standing that I have, and I'm going to do what's right.

I already know that in this world I'm going to face trouble, so there isn't any sense in crying about it. Imagine a running back in a football game. The quarterback hands him the ball. He hits the hole and they tackle him. He gets up crying and comes back to the huddle. The quarterback asks, "What's wrong?" The running back sobs, "They tackled me!" All the linemen and the other players look at him as if to say, "What's wrong with you? Getting tackled is part of the game."

Maybe in the 'hood where you grew up, there were certain basketball games you just didn't get into. When you saw the guys who were playing, you knew, "I'm not ready for that yet." You were too light to be going in underneath the basket. You needed to stay out in backcourt and pass that ball. You didn't dare go in. Maybe you knew that when you played on certain courts in certain areas of town, you were going to have to fight to get out. So you just went there ready. All I'm saying is, when you understood the rules, you didn't flinch when things went bad.

It is the same in life. The Bible says you're going to have some difficulty, so there's no sense in crying when trouble comes. You're a man. You may have to wade through some water, but that's okay. You're an overcomer. You've been created to overcome this.

25

When I encounter trouble, my attitude is totally different from what it used to be. Today, my family is going to have peace because I'm with them. They've seen me fight battles in the past, and they know I don't give out under pressure. So I can hold Momma real close and tell her, "Baby, it's going to be alright."

The Battle Plan

To come out of trouble, here are seven things we need to do. This is my battle plan.

1. *Cultivate a vision beyond the trouble I'm in.* Get the vision of another day. The Bible says that Jesus, for the joy that was set before Him, endured the cross (Heb. 12:2). I can endure any hardship if my focus isn't on the hard time but on what happens when I get through it.

2. *Choose victorious believers to teach me how to overcome.* In other words, I need to link up with some other victorious believers. Hebrews 6:12 says, "That ye be not slothful, but followers of them who through faith and patience inherit the promises." I need somebody to teach me the battle plan. No good army throws a warrior onto the battlefield without giving him basic training. I need to hook up with some victorious folks. I need to analyze the people I'm around, because if they're not victory-minded, I don't want to be around them. I need to make sure that I gravitate to people who believe in winning.

3. *Choose to voice my breakthrough in the middle of trouble.* In the midst of what I'm going through, I need to say that I'm coming out. I don't wait until I get out of trouble to say that. I prophesy my way out. I tell people, "I'm coming out. You just wait and see."

Mark 11:23–24 says, "For verily I say unto you, That whosoever shall say unto this mountain, Be thou removed, and be thou cast into the sea; and shall not doubt in his heart, but shall believe that those things which he saith shall come to pass; he shall have whatsoever he saith. Therefore I say unto you, What things soever ye desire, when ye pray, believe that ye receive them, and ye shall have them." Faith comes by hearing (Rom. 10:17), but faith is released by the words of my mouth. I have to be bold enough not to be intimidated by circumstances and declare that I'm coming out of the trouble I'm in.

More than 20 years ago, all the members of the church I was pastoring left. I told all the preachers I knew, "You just wait and see. That doesn't mean anything. What really matters hasn't changed. God's promise hasn't changed."

4. *Choose victorious behavior based on the Word of God, not on my feelings.*Second Corinthians 5:7 says, "For we walk by faith, not by sight." I choose to act like I'm going to win. Luke 5:17–26 tells the story of a paralyzed man who was lowered by his friends through the roof down to where Jesus was teaching. Verse 20 says, "When he saw their faith...." Those men had a victorious attitude. I need to have a victorious swagger about me. I have to walk as if victory is mine. I don't need any pity. Sympathy isn't going to get me out of my problem.

The scripture says for us to be "in nothing terrified by our adversaries" (Phil. 1:28). To paraphrase the thought, not being afraid of the devil sends him the message that he's going down. My confidence is not based on me; my confidence is based on what God told me and what He promised me. So if I believe I'm coming through the trouble, I don't have to act like I'm a failure, because I'm not. What you see me going through is only temporary. I've got winning on my mind.

5. *Consecrate a vow blessing for favor through a seed faith offering.* Psalm 50:14–15 says, "Offer unto God thanksgiving; and pay thy vows unto the most High: And call upon me in the day of trouble: I will deliver thee, and thou shalt glorify me." Now when a preacher starts talking about an offering, most people think everything he's said up until then has been just to get that offering. They think the preacher's trying to get their money. But if you think that, you're missing it. I can show you all through the Bible that when men wanted to win, they gave God an offering. They offered up a gift to Him for wisdom and for favor on their lives. When I go through any situation, I know that my victory is in my seed.

6. *Choose to vigorously bless the Lord for progressive results.* Hebrews 13:15 says, "By him therefore let us offer the sacrifice of praise to God continually, that is, the fruit of our lips giving thanks to his name." In other words, when I see the first little sign of things changing, I start rejoicing.

Let's say you're believing for better income, and you get a nickel-an-hour raise on your job. Don't curse the nickel! Your faith is starting to work! I know you'd rather have a five-dollar-an-hour raise, but at least you got a nickel. But most people start cursing the nickel. They start complaining, "Here I am, believing God for a raise, and all I get is a nickel an hour. A nickel! Five cents! How am I supposed to make it on that?" Oh no! You should be saying, "Praise the Lord! I got a nickel! That means I've opened a channel. Things are changing. Thank You, Lord!"

7. *Choose to volunteer beyond your victory to help others.* In other words, I hold my course and make a commitment that not only am I going to be a winner, but I'm going to do everything I can to help others win.

Trouble Can Damage Self-Esteem

If I don't handle trouble right, then the devil has a way of using trouble to damage my self-esteem. With damaged self-esteem, I'm no good to myself, to my family, or to the kingdom of God. So the devil's ultimate aim in trouble is to get me off the playing field. He wants me to be my own worst enemy.

If the devil can get you to talk down to yourself, he can go home. He'll try to get you to pull yourself into a bottomless pit of despair over your troubles. He wants to get you talking about how bad life is. He wants you saying, "Why me? Why does it always happen to me? Things are never going to be right. Something must be wrong with me." If the devil can get you to down yourself, he doesn't have to do it. He can go somewhere else.

The devil knows trouble can cause you to lose confidence not only in God but also in yourself. Knowing this, you have to know how to properly evaluate and protect your self-esteem—who you are. Self-esteem is how a man views himself, values himself, and validates himself. A man's self-esteem affects his behavior, his beliefs, and how he bonds with others. Your self-esteem is vitally important. The story of Gideon in the Bible illustrates that poor self-esteem can keep you from doing what God wants you to do.

Gideon had a problem with self-esteem. He and his brothers had been in a battle, and his brothers had died. That bothered him—it scarred him. So when the Angel of the Lord appeared to him in Judges chapter 6, Gideon said to him, "If the Lord is with us, then why are we in the trouble we're in?" His whole attitude was negative because he had gone through trouble and didn't get victory. But the angel told him, "It isn't over. I've come to help level the playing field." Before it was all over in Judges chapter 8, Gideon had his foot on the necks of the guys who killed his brothers. Gideon asked them what kind of men they had killed at Tabor. They told him, "They looked kind of like you." Gideon said, "They were my brothers. And since you killed them there, I'm killing you now." But before Gideon could get to that point, God had to work on his self-esteem.

God wants me to love myself and believe in myself. He wants me to understand that I'm chosen royalty, a new creature in Christ Jesus. He wants me to get beyond all the excuses and the things that the devil does to tear me down. God wants me to know that the Kingdom way of evaluating my worth is different from the world's way.

People in the world value themselves based on possessions, position, proficiency, and presentation. We've been trained to value other people that way. We esteem them highly and put ourselves in a lower state just because we don't have what they have, we're not where they're at, we can't do what they can do, and we don't look as good as they do. But the Bible tells us not to be conformed to the world, but to be transformed by the renewing of our minds (Rom. 12:2). We have to have a paradigm shift in our thinking. Something has to change in our thoughts about ourselves so we can always feel good about ourselves, whether we have a thousand dollars in the bank or we're in the red.

Look at something Jesus said in Luke chapter 12.

Luke 12:15

15 And he said unto them, Take heed, and beware of covetousness: for a man's life consisteth not in the abundance of the things which he possesseth.

Jesus said here that in God's sight a man is not measured by his stuff. That's a major shift away from how our society thinks, but you have to make that shift because this is truth. The Bible says you don't judge a man, including yourself, by your stuff. You'll never be able to walk among trees if you see yourself as a twig.

I have to choose to remind myself that my value is not based on my stuff; my value is based on the price paid for me. Jesus became my Substitute, and my potential is based on what He can do through me. I'm not putting down education. Praise the Lord for education. But God can do through me what education can't teach me. So I'm not handicapped because I didn't get a degree. I don't have to take a back seat because I didn't go to college. I am God's workmanship—His handiwork (Eph. 2:10). I can do all things through Christ which strengthens me (Phil. 4:13). But I have to believe that. If I believe that, I won't let myself be put down.

Look in First Corinthians chapter 6.

1 Corinthians 6:20
20 For ye are bought with a price: therefore glorify God in your body, and in your spirit, which are God's.

The bottom line is, the price that was paid for me is the same price that was paid for you. To the degree that I understand that, I will respect every man as a man. You see, my respect for a man is how I measure the man. I don't measure you by your stuff. You may have a nice car and nice shoes, but that's not the measuring stick God wants me to use. The measuring stick that God gave me to measure you by is the blood of Jesus. The blood that saved you and brought you up is the same blood that saved me and brought me up. The same price was paid for us both.

If you can understand this truth and saturate yourself with it, it will transform your life. You will start seeing yourself differently, and folks will start treating you differently because you determine how people treat you.

Look in Hebrews chapter 13.

Hebrews 13:5

5 Let your conversation [that's your lifestyle] be without covetousness; and be content with such things as ye have: for he hath said, I will never leave thee, nor forsake thee.

God said His relationship with you has nothing to do with what you have or don't have. He has committed to be with you always. Look at this verse in *The Amplified Bible.*

Hebrews 13:5

5 Let your character or moral disposition be free from love of money [including greed, avarice, lust, and craving for earthly possessions] and be satisfied with your present [circumstances and with what you have]; for He [God] Himself has said, I will not in any way fail you nor give you up nor leave you without support. [I will] not, [I will] not, [I will] not in any degree leave you helpless nor forsake nor let [you] down (relax My hold on you)! [Assuredly not!]

If you can make the shift in your mind, you can look any man in the eye because you understand that God is committed to you. This is how you change—not by saying, "When I get a new car, they're going to respect me." No, when you get a new revelation of who you are in Jesus, then you get respect.

3

A Man and
.His Mouth

In the last chapter, we looked at the inevitability of trouble in life, and our need to make plans to handle trouble. In this chapter, we're going to see how powerful our words are.

The Bible says something about this in Genesis chapter 2.

Genesis 2:19

19 And out of the ground the LORD God formed every beast of the field, and every fowl of the air; and brought them unto Adam to see what he would call them: and whatsoever Adam called every living creature, that was the name thereof.

One translation says, "Whatever Adam called each living creature, that was its name." In other words, God said, "Adam, whatever you call this animal, that's what it will be." Adam's words were powerful, and so are our words today. The words we speak will release either faith or fear into our lives. Unfortunately, most of us grew up in churches where nobody taught us about the power of our words. My goal in this chapter is to impress upon you how powerful your words are. Once you come to respect this principle, you must learn how to maximize your words so you can transform your world. Your words mean something.

God established a principle with Adam: "Whatever you call it, that's what it's going to be." And it's the same for you.

The Bible teaches us that death and life are in the power of the tongue (Prov. 18:21). So as a man, if I'm going to master life, I must master my tongue. I must learn the power of my words, and I must know how and when to speak, and what to say.

Jesus reinforced what God said to Adam about this. In Mark chapter 11 Jesus talked about faith.

> Mark 11:22–23
>
> 22 And Jesus answering saith unto them, Have faith in God.
>
> 23 For verily I say unto you, That whosoever shall say unto this mountain, Be thou removed, and be thou cast into the sea; and shall not doubt in his heart, but shall believe that those things which he saith shall come to pass; he shall have whatsoever he saith.

A man will have whatever he says. That's a biblical principle. Faith comes by hearing, but faith is released by the words of my mouth. To the degree that I understand this powerful principle, I will monitor my mouth.

Faith in the context of this chapter is a spiritual principle that taps into the creative power of God which is available to every man. Through your faith, you can tap into God's creative power and transform conditions, circumstances, and situations in the natural realm that God has given you authority over.

I have authority over my house, so I can use my faith in my household and bring transformation, but the principles and process of faith have to be learned. We learn them through others who understand them. We see this in Hebrews chapter 6.

Hebrews 6:12

12 That ye be not slothful, but followers of them who through faith and patience inherit the promises.

You have to link up with somebody who's walking in the manifestation of the promise so you can learn from them. For every promise, principle, and prophecy, there is a faith process to bring it to pass.

I grew up in church hearing about faith, but I didn't know how to use faith. I knew the term *faith,* but I did not know how to operate in the God-kind of faith until God let me get close enough to a man of faith to learn how it works. My mentor is Dr. Frederick K.C. Price, the godfather of faith. I got close enough to him to glean from him. I learned how I was to operate in faith by watching him operate in faith.

I like to give testimonies because I want you to see how I exercise faith in real-life situations. I'm a pastor, and people often ask me what I did when there were 300 people in my church and 277 left, leaving me with only 23 members. It didn't bother me. I wasn't focused on the folks who left. Obviously, they didn't want to stay. If I had worried about them leaving, I would have missed the opportunity to minister to the army of 23 that I still had. Everybody didn't leave.

If I believe the Word of God that says, "If thou canst believe, all things are possible to him that believeth" (Mark 9:23), then I have to believe I can do what God told me to do, starting with the 23. I can't start thinking, *Oh Lord, what am I going to do?* I don't think like most folks do. My thinking has been transformed by the Word. I walk by faith and not by sight (2 Cor. 5:7). So I don't let what I see bother me. It's a distraction. If I allow it to affect me, it can, but if I choose not to allow it to affect me, it can't.

That's what the Bible says about Abraham. He considered not what he saw (Rom. 4:19). Oh, he was aware that he could not have sex with his wife. He was aware that both of their bodies were sexually dead, but he didn't let that sway him in what he chose to believe.

You have to choose to believe the Word of God. You are going to believe something. Right now you are believing something that somebody told you. You may believe that it's hard for a black man to get a break or get ahead in life because somebody told you that. I just made a switch one day. I said, "I'm not going to believe any of that, because it's not in the Bible. I choose to believe only what the Bible says." I made a choice. And you have made a choice to believe something. Now, you just have to choose that you're going to believe what the Word of God says.

So the Bible tells us to be "followers of them who through faith and patience inherit the promises" (Heb. 6:12). I am to model the faith of others. When I saw my pastor, Dr. Price, I'd check him out. I watched how he handled things. I was learning how to talk the faith talk and walk the faith walk. I watched how he received the offering and how he responded when the budget wasn't met. I was sitting there, but I was gleaning all I could. I didn't have to know him up close. A lot of people don't understand that. I followed Dr. Price for many years and never got close to him. I went to all the crusades I could and just sat there and checked him out. I was taking notes.

Then one day, Dr. Price was in a crusade and I think Dr. Betty, his wife, was getting ready to have a meeting. Dr. Price wanted to have lunch with some of the pastors who were there, and somebody told him, "Ask that little guy to come. He's always in the meetings." So he sent somebody to get me. But before I ever met Dr. Price personally I learned how to walk by faith and discipline my emotions. By watching his example, I learned not to be moved by what I see but only by what I believe. But getting to that point was a process.

Number One: Ask the Father in Jesus' Name

Here is the process of faith. First, *ask the Father in Jesus' Name.* Jesus said, "What things soever ye desire, when ye pray, believe that ye receive them, and ye shall have them" (Mark 11:24). Faith begins where the will of God is known. Jesus said the following:

> John 16:23
> 23 And in that day ye shall ask me nothing. Verily, verily, I say unto you, Whatsoever ye shall ask the Father in my name, he will give it you.

So in a prayer of petition, I am to ask the Father in Jesus' Name for what I desire. Now look at these verses in First John chapter 5.

> 1 John 5:14–15
> 14 And this is the confidence that we have in him, that, if we ask any thing according to his will, he heareth us:

15 And if we know that he hear us, whatsoever we ask, we know that we have the petitions that we desired of him.

The will of God is the Word of God. So I'm to ask according to His Word. When I pray according to God's Word, I already know what the will of God is, so I don't have to say, "if it be Thy will." I know from God's Word that it's His will for me to be blessed (Ps. 5:12) and rich (2 Cor. 8:9) and to have all my needs met (Phil. 4:19). I know it's God's will for me to walk in health (Ps. 103:3; 3 John 2). I already know that. I don't have to close my prayer with the religious statement "if it be Thy will." I already know His will.

Some people will say, "I wouldn't talk to God like that." Well, they don't have the relationship with Him that I have, nor do they have the results. I already know what His will is. He told me what it is. And I hope you can get the same attitude.

Number Two: Believe You Receive

So first, I ask the Father in Jesus' Name, and I ask according to His Word, which is His will. Second, *I believe I receive what I ask for.*

Believing is an act of your will. You can will to believe, and you can will not to believe. The Bible says in John chapter 20 that Thomas was not with the other Apostles when Jesus appeared to them after His resurrection. When they told Thomas later that they'd seen the Lord, Thomas said, "I don't believe that. Unless I see the nail holes in his hands and put my finger into those holes and put my hand into the hole in his side, I will not believe" (John 20:25). Thomas willed not to believe what the other Apostles told him. Believing is always a matter of your will. Whether you believe or don't believe is up to you.

The Bible says that eight days later Thomas was with the other Apostles and the doors were shut, and Jesus walked in and said, "Hey, Thomas, come here! Reach out your finger and put it in the hole in My hand. Reach out your hand and put it in the hole in My side, and be not faithless but believing" (John 20:27). Jesus was saying here that if you need physical evidence to set your will to accept something, then that is not biblical believing. *Biblical believing is accepting something as fact without any evidence from the sensory realm.* It is accepting something as a fact based solely on the evidence of God's Word. You can choose to believe without any sensory realm evidence. You're already doing that. You just need to take it up to another level.

You may ask, "How am I believing in something without evidence from my senses?" Well, do you believe in Heaven? If you do, have you ever been there? If you haven't, you've accepted something as fact without any sensory realm evidence. That's biblical believing. The only evidence I need is the Word of God. The Word says, "Faith is the substance of things hoped for, the evidence of things not seen" (Heb. 11:1), and "Faith cometh by hearing, and hearing by the word of God" (Rom. 10:17). So faith and the Word of God are somewhat synonymous. Therefore, I could read Hebrews 11:1 this way:

"The Word of God is the substance of things hoped for; the Word of God is the evidence of things not seen." What I know about the unseen arena, I get from the Word. I choose by an act of my will to believe it and accept it as fact, even though I have no sensory realm evidence for it.

If I have credibility with you and I tell you that at my house I have a Rolls Royce, you'll believe me. Without having to go see it, you'll start telling folks, "You know, Dr. Hilliard has a Rolls." If you trust me to tell the truth, you'll say that without any sensory realm evidence. You haven't seen that Rolls Royce. You haven't sat in it or ridden in it. But because a person of credibility told you, you believe it.

You do the same thing with the Word of God. He Who cannot lie has made some amazing promises to you, and you have to choose to accept them as fact. You may not know how He's going to cause them to come to pass, but He said it and you choose to believe it. You believe it to the point that I can't talk you out of it. You believe it to the point that even if it doesn't look like those promises are coming to pass, it doesn't matter. I still can't shake you, because you have set your will to believe.

All Thomas was saying when the other Apostles told him that they had seen the Lord was, "My criterion for believing is sensory realm evidence." Jesus said, "Thomas, you have to change your criterion from having to use your five physical senses to verify something to just believing it on the basis of My Word. Blessed are those who have not seen and yet have believed."

Number Three: Confess Your Faith

So I have asked the Father in Jesus' Name based on the Word of God, and I have believed that I have received what I've asked for. The third step in the process of faith is, *I must confess what I believe.* I have to have the boldness to say it, to use my mouth to release faith in the earth through my words.

Jesus said, "…the words that I speak unto you, they are spirit, and they are life" (John 6:63). We must understand that our words are not just sounds that vibrate on the eardrum. Our words have spiritual power. We release spiritual power, or faith power, in the earth through our words.

When you open your mouth and say something, things start happening in the spirit world. How do we know that? The Bible tells us. According to the Bible, God created two arenas: a spirit world and a natural world, and He created the natural world from the spirit world (see Genesis chapter 1; Heb. 11:3). That means spiritual things have preeminence over natural things.

God, Who is a Spirit, was here first. The spirit realm was here first. And from the spirit realm God spoke the natural world into existence. That means the natural world is dependent on the spirit world; the spirit world isn't depending on the natural. Everything I see around me is a product of what happened first spiritually. And I'm a spirit being living in a physical body. That gives me the ability to function in two arenas. I can function in the physical world because I am a natural man. And I can function in the spirit world because I am a spirit man. So there are spiritual laws that I can function in which give me an advantage in life.

Angels Are Waiting for Your Words

When you speak God's Word, angels start moving. They're standing by waiting for you to do that, because when you start speaking God's Word, they get their orders. Psalm 103 refers to that.

Psalm 103:20
20 Bless the LORD, ye his angels, that excel in strength, that do his commandments, hearkening unto the voice of his word.

When I start speaking in line with God's Word, my angels— spirit beings who have been sent to help me—begin to move. When I speak God's Word, demonic forces are traumatized and restrained. The Bible says of Jesus, "…he cast out the spirits with his word" (Matt. 8:16). With my words I do business in the spirit realm against demonic forces. Don't let the devil do all the talking. When he talks to you, talk God's Word back to him. Don't just sit there and say, "Uh-huh. Uh-huh." No! When the devil talked to Jesus, Jesus talked back to him. And what did Jesus say? "It is written, it is written, it is written" (see Matt. 4:3–11).

When I speak faith-filled words, the force of faith is released in the spirit realm. I have to see faith as a hammer. Every time I speak the Word, that hammer pounds against whatever would keep me from what God has promised me until I drive the obstacle and the resistance out of my life.

Faith-Filled Words Carry Spiritual Authority

I release spiritual authority with faith-filled words. In other words, the authority that I have is released by the words of my mouth. So how do I make this faith confession? How do I control my mouth? I do it on purpose. I don't deny the existence of a problem when I see it. I don't deny what is going on. No, I release faith on purpose. Jesus taught me how to release my faith. So I choose to make a faith confession on purpose. A faith confession is a statement that agrees with the Word of God regardless of circumstances. I know that the only way I can license God to get involved in my situation is if I say that His Word is the truth regardless of what things look like.

So I choose to call those things which be not as though they were. It's a choice. Now I could choose to talk about how bad situations are, but that won't change them. In Genesis chapter 1, when God saw that it was dark, He didn't say, "Ooh, look at the darkness!" He said, "Let there be light!" So in dark situations in my life, I must choose not to talk about the darkness; I must choose to talk about God's promise. I talk about the light. I have nothing to lose and everything to gain.

When I was just starting to walk by faith, people told me, "There's something wrong with you. How can you say that you're prosperous and successful?" I didn't have anything to lose. I was already broke. My car was pitiful. My finances were messed up. I didn't have a problem going through the house talking to my furniture. I didn't have any money to buy any more furniture. When I talked to it in line with God's Word, at least I felt I was doing something about the situation. I walked up to that chair and said, "I call you replaced. You're a raggedy chair. You are veneer over particle board. You are not even real wood. You are not God's best for me or for my family. The Bible says wealth and riches ought to be in my house" (Ps. 112:1,3). I used to walk out to my car and say, "You are not God's best for me, and you'd better start." This is what you have to do. What do you have to lose by transforming your mouth?

We have been conditioned and trained to talk negatively. When you start talking negatively, people chime in with you and agree with you. If you start saying how hard it is and how much things cost, they'll say, "Yeah, it's hard. Did you see the price of gas?" But if you say, "I declare every need met. I have abundance. I walk in God's best," people will say, "Well you don't have to brag about it and put everybody else down." I'm not putting everybody else down. I'm just saying that my God supplies all my need. "Oh, you're one of those Christians, huh?" But as long as I talked negatively, I was all right. I was one of the gang.

God taught Abraham to do this. God changed his name from Abram to Abraham to teach him this principle of calling things that be not as though they were. Before I had revelation about this, I'd wonder, "Why is God going around in the Bible changing people's names? Doesn't He like their names? Why would He do that?" Well, God does everything for a reason. He did not change Abram's name to Abraham just because He didn't like the sound of Abram. He was teaching him faith.

God had to teach Abram faith because even though He had made Abraham a promise, He could not deliver on that promise without Abraham's participation in faith. God had to teach Abraham faith so He'd be justified in delivering the promise. Faith comes by hearing, and since Abraham had heard the Word, God had to teach him the next level—that faith is released by the words of your mouth. God had to teach Abraham how to speak in faith. So He changed his name from

Abram to Abraham, which meant "father of nations." So even before Abraham became the father of nations, he was calling himself the father of nations.

God heard faith, and that authorized Him to get involved. He changed Abraham's wife's name from Sarai to Sarah, which means "mother of many." So this old woman who wasn't functioning sexually walked around calling herself the mother of many. Her confession transformed her body to the point that Abraham took her to one country and the king saw her and said he wanted her. You know she couldn't have looked like some dried-up prune.

When I make a faith confession, that confession has to be personal—it has to be in the present tense—and I have to say it persistently.

Number Four: Demonstrate Your Faith

When I operate in faith, I ask the Father in Jesus' Name; I believe that I receive when I pray; I make faith confessions; and then *I demonstrate my faith.* I act in agreement with what the Word of God promises me and with what I'm saying. If I'm saying I believe every need is met, I can't walk around with my head down.

I have five justifiable expectations when I'm in faith. Number one, I expect a plan of action. Number two, I expect the favor of God. Number three, I expect the wisdom of God. Number four, I expect a miracle. And number five, I expect strength to endure until things change.

Look in John chapter 1. John the Baptist was out in the wilderness preaching. He looked kind of strange, and the religious leaders wanted to know who he was, so they sent people to ask him.

John 1:22–23

22 Then said they unto him, Who art thou? that we may give an answer to them that sent us. What sayest thou of thyself?

23 He said, I am the voice of one crying in the wilderness, Make straight the way of the Lord, as said the prophet Esaias.

John the Baptist chose to define himself by the Word. He could have said, "Go back and tell them that my daddy is Zachariah and my momma is Elizabeth," but that's not what he chose to do. He chose to say what the Word of God said about him. By doing that he was releasing faith into his situation and licensing God to operate.

That's what you have to choose to do, no matter what things looks like. Now, it's easy to say what God's Word says about you as long as things in your life aren't bad. But when things get really bad, it can be easy to give up.

I remember when the finance company repossessed my car. My faith hadn't produced enough money to pay the note, and they hooked my car up and towed it away. All I had to drive was the church's 66-passenger bus. But I didn't throw my faith away, because it wasn't over. It wasn't the end of my world. That wasn't the only car left. The car companies were still making cars every day. I didn't shed any tears. Yeah, I couldn't pay the note and I had to give the man his car back, but that didn't keep me from confessing God's Word. I didn't change my confession. Everywhere I went in that bus, I confessed, "I'm not moved by what I see. I'm only moved by what I believe." I drove down the highway shifting gears and confessing the Word.

You have to choose to stick with it. I see a lot of people start right and then quit. I tell them, "No. You have too much invested. Don't quit now." When things get tough and it looks like it's not happening, you still work and do everything you can in the natural, but you keep your mouth on it. You keep speaking what God says, and you keep your faith on His promise. The scripture says, "Let us hold fast the profession of our faith without wavering; (for he is faithful that promised)" (Heb. 10:23).

When my church first started, people all over the state of Texas laughed at me. They'd say, "Hilliard has gone off the deep end. That boy is crazy. All he's doing is teaching. He really believes that people are going to come and listen to him." But that didn't bother me, because God didn't say, "According to *their* faith, be it unto you." He said, "According to *your* faith, be it unto you" (Matt. 9:29). I refuse to let somebody else define what my faith can get for me. The bottom line is, nobody is laughing anymore, and I'm not driving the bus anymore. I'm driving what I require. My faith has produced what I require.

Maybe you can't handle that. You're driving the kind of car you require. Your faith has produced it. When you learn to raise your requirement, you can drive a better car. Your faith will produce what you require. And if you give God a bigger bag, He'll fill it.

4

A Man and
His Morals

My goal in this chapter is to instruct you in righteous and holy living according to the moral code of the God of the Scriptures. We'll begin by looking at a few verses from First Peter chapter 1.

1 Peter 1:13–16

13 Wherefore gird up the loins of your mind, be sober, and hope to the end for the grace that is to be brought unto you at the revelation of Jesus Christ;

14 As obedient children, not fashioning yourselves according to the former lusts in your ignorance:

15 But as he which hath called you is holy, so be ye holy in all manner of conversation;

16 Because it is written, Be ye holy; for I am holy.

Now let's look at these verses from *The Amplified Bible.*

1 Peter 1:13-16

13 So brace up your minds; be sober (circumspect, morally alert); set your hope wholly and unchangeably on the grace

(divine favor) that is coming to you when Jesus Christ (the Messiah) is revealed.

14 [Live] as children of obedience [to God]; do not conform yourselves to the evil desires [that governed you] in your former ignorance [when you did not know the requirements of the Gospel].

15 But as the One Who called you is holy, you yourselves also be holy in all your conduct and manner of living.

16 For it is written, You shall be holy, for I am holy.

We live in a day when morality changes based on what is popular. This is called social morality. But I'm going to focus on righteous morality based on the Word of God.

When I was born again, my mind and body did not change. What changed was my spirit, which was made alive to God. It is His plan for me to do something with my body and my mind, but I have to know what He wants me to do. Unfortunately, many times people in church think that when they confess Jesus Christ as Lord, that is the silver bullet for righteousness. In other words, they think that now that they've become Christians, all their old desires will go away. They think that everything they used to do, they're not going to want to do anymore. But that's not the case.

With many people, when they get saved, they don't go to some of the places they used to go to. It's not that they *don't want* to go. They just don't go.

There is a spiritual antidote—really, it's what I'd call a vaccine—for sexual obsessions and perversions. The Word of God addresses addictive behavior of all kinds, and through the principles of deliverance, every man can be set free.

We're talking about holiness—about living right. Everybody wants the preacher to live right, but living right is not just for the preacher. Preachers ought to live right, but *every man* is supposed to live right. We see this in First Thessalonians chapter 4.

> 1 Thessalonians 4:6–7
>
> 6 That no man go beyond and defraud his brother in any matter: because that the Lord is the avenger of all such, as we also have forewarned you and testified.
>
> 7 For God hath not called us unto uncleanness, but unto holiness.

We see here that God has called us to holiness. Now as I said, the new birth changed my spirit, but it didn't change my mind. If I had a perverted mind before I was born again, I had a perverted mind after I was born again. If my body was out of order and in the habit of yielding to lusting desires and cravings before my new birth, then that was still the case after my new birth. Unfortunately, nobody likes to talk about this. So Christians go through life in bondage, but they don't have to. They can be free.

Weakness Can Be Overcome

Weakness to sin can be overcome. This weakness is manifested through our choices, but we must decide not to stay in that state. We must choose to live according to the Word of God. *It's a choice.* If you have not made that choice, I believe the Spirit of God wants to bring you to a place where you will make that choice today. I believe that today, some things in your life are going to change. Look in James chapter 1.

James 1:13–15

13 Let no man say when he is tempted, I am tempted of God: for God cannot be tempted with evil, neither tempteth he any man:

14 But every man is tempted, when he is drawn away of his own lust, and enticed.

15 Then when lust hath conceived, it bringeth forth sin: and sin, when it is finished, bringeth forth death.

Notice that verse 14 says every man is tempted when he is drawn away *of his own lust.* It's obvious that we can do something about this problem, otherwise, God wouldn't have mentioned it in His Word. We must understand that there is a real enemy. To face him successfully, the Bible tells me I have to get my thinking ready. God says, "Gird up the loins of your mind" (1 Pet. 1:13). So, *change for the believer is the product of human effort sustained by divine help.* God will not change me against my will. But if I desire to change and I make steps toward change, at that moment divine help comes into my life.

Luke chapter 22 relates Jesus' words to Peter about his coming temptation. It's important to know Satan's plan and the pitfalls that can derail a man. You have to know that you have a real enemy who desires to trip you up. He can't keep you out of Heaven, but he wants to keep you from having God's best. We must be consciously aware of this enemy without being consumed by thoughts that the devil is like the big, bad wolf. He isn't all he's cracked up to be. He's not "all of that."

By the time we get to Luke chapter 22, Jesus has been mentoring Peter for about three years. Now watch this.

Luke 22:31–32

31 And the Lord said, Simon, Simon, behold, Satan hath desired to have you, that he may sift you as wheat:

32 But I have prayed for thee, that thy faith fail not: and when thou art converted, strengthen thy brethren.

I like this scripture. Jesus is saying, "Even though I love you, Peter, I cannot protect you from the attack. The attack is going to come." But Jesus adds, "I have prayed for you, that your faith fail not." In others words, Jesus was telling Peter that he had what it took to win. And He added that he fully expected Peter to win, because He said, "And when you are converted, you owe it to your brothers to help them." In other words, Jesus was telling Peter not to let another brother struggle with something he had already struggled with.

So Jesus has confidence in your ability to win the battle against the addiction that you face. *Jesus has confidence in you.*

The Devil Attacks With Thoughts

The Bible is filled with stories of all kinds of attacks. These attacks occur in the arena of your thought life. That's where the devil shows up. He doesn't show up wearing a red suit and carrying a pitchfork. He shows up with thoughts. You have to understand how he works so you can make sure that he won't work his game successfully on you. He attacks men. He attacked Job. He attacked Jesus. He tries to steal the Word. He attacks with sickness and disease. He attacked Ananias and Sapphira. He attacked Judas. The devil is on a rampage, but he doesn't have to defeat you. You don't have to let him. Look in Ephesians chapter 6.

Ephesians 6:16

16 Above all, taking the shield of faith, wherewith ye shall be able to quench all the fiery darts of the wicked.

If you look at the context for this verse, you see that Paul is talking about putting on the whole armor of God, and the fiery darts here are thoughts. Think about your own life. Every bit of misbehavior you got into started with a thought. That thought may have been triggered by something you saw, but you had to take that thought and do something with it. That's why the devil plays his game in the arena of your mind. That's why the scripture, when it talks about holiness, says, "Gird up the loins of your mind" (1 Pet. 1:13). The devil starts there. And until you can get mentally strong, you can't fight.

It is said that 60 percent of men in the Body of Christ have some experience with pornography. That means you can take ten men out of any church, and six of them have had some experience with pornographic material. I really want you to be anchored in the Word as we look at this, because through the Word of God you can get free from any addiction. Look in James chapter 4.

James 4:7

7 Submit yourselves therefore to God. Resist the devil, and he will flee from you.

Now look at that same verse from *The Amplified Bible.*

James 4:7

7 So be subject to God. Resist the devil [stand firm against him], and he will flee from you.

First, we need to submit ourselves to God. We looked at that in Chapter 1 of this book. Then, we are to resist the devil, and he will flee.

How Does the Devil Play His Game?

Let's look now at how the devil plays his game. How does he come in and entice us? If we know how he plays his game, then when we see him playing that game on us, we can stop him. The devil uses music, friends, the media, and many other avenues to entice us.

Number one, *Satan challenges the existence of God.* Have you ever had the thought, *Is there really a God?* If you've been to college, you've had that thought, because when you get onto a college campus, that's often the first question you get hit with. When you get to college, you're outside of the cocoon of familiarity that you were raised up in. At college, you're exposed to people who haven't been to church and don't go to church. They couldn't care less about God or anything related to Him. The first thing they want to ask you is, "How do you know there's a God?" They force you to think in ways you've never had to think before.

Number two, *Satan challenges God's right to rule our lives.* He challenges God's right to tell us what to do. As we saw in Chapter 1, God has the right to rule over us. He created us, and to experience His best for our lives, we must obey Him.

Number three, *Satan magnifies the imperfections in visible authority.* Why? Because he's trying to get you to believe that you have a justifiable right not to do right. That's why you hear people say, "Well, the preacher did this, and the preacher didn't do that, and that isn't right!" The preacher is a visible representative of spiritual authority. If visible spiritual authority can be presented as not doing right, then another person can make an excuse for himself and say, "I don't need to do right either."

Number four, *Satan redefines those who love me as my enemies.* In other words, there are folks in my life who are trying to keep me on the right track. When the devil wants to entice me to misbehave, he redefines those folks in my mind as people who are trying to hold me back. Many a man got into trouble simply because he began to see his parents as his enemies. He thought, *They're trying to keep me from having fun.* But they were trying to keep him from going to jail, because he was running with the wrong crowd.

Number five, *Satan uses emotional triggers to provoke guilt, shame, and embarrassment.* If Satan can get you to begin to feel embarrassment, shame, or guilt about unfortunate circumstances in your life, whether past or present, whether caused by you or someone else, he has found an open door in your life to harass you. Constant thoughts like this create pressure that can weigh you down. You will start to feel unworthy and not care about what you do. His goal is to make you feel like there is no hope, so that you can act in a destructive manner that will negatively affect your life.

Number six, *Satan looks for unsurrendered areas in your flesh to exploit with temptation.* He knows every man's weakness. He knows them because of what the Bible calls iniquity and familiar spirits. He knows what he tricked your daddy and your granddaddy with. He knows the sin line that runs in your family. It isn't women, drugs, or gambling for everybody, but he's got your number.

Number seven, *Satan minimizes the impact of the consequences of sin.* He tries to get you thinking that you can handle it, whether it's drinking, women, gambling, or anything else. No matter what sin it is, he begins to minimize the consequences.

Number eight, *Satan isolates you from righteous influences.* He wants to get you off by yourself, because once he does that and he's the only one talking to you, he's got you.

Number nine, *Satan sets you up to push you over the edge into perverted action.* He tries to frustrate you to the point where you don't care what you do. Have you ever gotten to the point where you did something because at that moment you didn't care? If you had been in your right mind, you never would have done it, but the devil pushed you so far and got you so frustrated that you said, "Oh, what the heck. I might as well do it."

Number ten, *Satan helps you fabricate counterfeit spiritual directions to justify your rebellion and disloyalty.* In other words, you're misbehaving and doing something you know you shouldn't do, but you say, "God knows my heart." That sounds really spiritual, doesn't it? You're messing around, "but the Lord knows my heart."

One pastor I ministered to had been unfaithful to his wife, and his ministry had gone haywire. His church membership would build up and then he'd have an affair with a woman in the church. The woman would promise him she wouldn't tell anybody, but she always talked about it, because, you see, she'd gotten the king. She had to brag about it. Then his wife and children would be hurt and the church would get mad and his membership would fall off. This happened more than once.

This man came to my office and wanted help. As we were talking, he said, "I don't know why God made me like this! I didn't even enjoy it!" He put the responsibility for what he was doing on God. I said, "Hold it. Time out. James 1:14 says that a man sins when he is drawn away of his own lust. Don't you try to put this on God. Hebrews 11:25 says that sin is pleasurable. Every time you got together with one of those women, you enjoyed it. So don't sit here and tell me you didn't enjoy it, because you wouldn't have kept doing it if you didn't."

My point is, Satan tries to get you to spiritualize things. I've heard some men say, "God didn't mind David having other women, because He told him, 'You could have had this one and that one, but you should have left this other one alone'" (2 Sam. 12:8–9). That's foolishness. The Bible tells us to live holy lives (Rom. 12:1; 1 Pet. 1:15–16).

What Do I Do When I Feel Trapped?

So what do you do when you feel trapped in sin? How do you get out? I can beat you over the head for a week about not sinning, but you already know you're not supposed to commit adultery. Really, you almost don't need the Bible to tell you that. If you told one woman that you would love her and be with her forever, you really don't even need the Bible to know that it's wrong to violate that covenant by sleeping with somebody else. You don't need the Bible to tell you that sexual perversions like messing with children are wrong. Just ask yourself, "Would I want somebody messing with my children?" What would you do if somebody was exploiting and taking advantage of your child? I don't even need to read you a scripture. You'd pray that the police would get them before you caught them.

So if you've gotten caught up in a sin, how do you get out of it? There's so much shame attached to these addictive sin behaviors, and they lead to such a poor self-image, that guys hide for years and never step up and get free. Jesus said that He came "to preach deliverance to the captives" (Luke 4:18). He came to set the captives free, and that means free of whatever you got caught up in. You can get caught up in things, not intending to get addicted to them. We're going to see that process, and the solution, in Romans chapter 7.

> Romans 7:18–23
>
> 18 For I know that in me (that is, in my flesh,) dwelleth no good thing: for to will is present with me; but how to perform that which is good I find not.
>
> 19 For the good that I would I do not: but the evil which I would not, that I do.
>
> 20 Now if I do that I would not, it is no more I that do it, but sin that dwelleth in me.
>
> 21 I find then a law, that, when I would do good, evil is present with me.
>
> 22 For I delight in the law of God after the inward man:
>
> 23 But I see another law in my members, warring against the law of my mind, and bringing me into captivity to the law of sin which is in my members.

Paul writes in verse 23 about how what his body wants wars against what his born-again spirit wants, and his body brings him into captivity to the law of sin. In the next verse, he's looking for the way out.

Romans 7:24

24 O wretched man that I am! who shall deliver me from the body of this death?

What an awesome revelation! Paul didn't ask, "What can deliver me?" He asked *who!* He understood that his freedom was going to come through a relationship. Now watch this.

Romans 7:25–8:1

25 I thank God through Jesus Christ our Lord. So then with the mind I serve the law of God; but with the flesh the law of sin.

1 There is therefore now no condemnation to them which are in Christ Jesus, who walk not after the flesh, but after the Spirit.

Here in Romans 8:1, Paul points out that the key to winning the constant battle between your spirit and your flesh is to walk in the Spirit.

Now, the sexual misbehavior that is prevalent all around us results from a deception. A deception is a mistaken conviction based on misinformation. And this mistaken conviction produces misbehavior. You have to understand that you can get victory over addictive behavior, whether it's gambling, violence, beating your wife, pornography, or anything else. You can get free from surfing the Internet, buying the books, going to the peep shows, and fantasizing about somebody else while you're having sex with your wife. The good part here is that you can be free.

The sex drive is one of the strongest passions men have. It was given to us to guarantee procreation. But satanic exploitation of that sex drive opens the door for misbehavior. It starts with a choice.

I was driving with another guy in the car one day and he asked me about all the pretty women in my church. He asked, "Do you ever mess with any of them?" I said, "No, no, no." He said, "I don't understand how you do that. How do you have all those pretty women around you and not mess with any of them?"

Well, while we were driving I had to stop at a store. I left him in the car, but on purpose I left some money on the console. When I came back, the money was still there. So I asked him, "Did you see that money I left there?"

"Yeah, yeah, I saw it."

"That's some serious money. Wouldn't you want that?"

"Yeah."

"Couldn't you use that?"

"Yeah."

"So how come you didn't take it?"

"It wasn't mine."

"You didn't have to pray about it?"

"Naw," he said. "It wasn't mine. That belonged to you."

"Well, that's the same decision I made about those women. Another man's wife belongs to him. She isn't mine. I don't care how good she looks. And another man's daughter isn't my wife. I have no business looking at her. I don't have to pray about that. I made a covenant with my eyes" (Job 31:1).

The Bible says, "Gird up the loins of your mind." Some people want to spiritualize things, but a lot of things in life just come down to a decision.

Now, I admit that some problems can go deeper. You can toy with sin and eventually it can get a grip on your soul. Some people in the Bible were ruled by a compulsion they could not control that was orchestrated by the devil. For example, there was the lunatic who lived in the graveyard (Mark 5:1–20). People would tie him up with chains and bring him to the graveyard, then he'd break the chains and run into the wilderness. That's compulsive behavior. There also was the man whose son was an epileptic (Mark 9:17–29). The man told Jesus that the boy often was thrown into the fire and into the water. An evil spirit drove the boy to do that.

So it is possible for Satan to encroach on your life to the point where you are driven to do things. Something has become an obsession. Getting free of that takes more than just a decision, because that thing has now rooted itself in your soul. But you still can be free.

We'll deal with other problems besides sex, but you've got to understand how strong the sex drive is, and how the devil tries to use that against you. Sexual messages are all around you. It's hard to find a decent movie that doesn't have sexual overtones or blatant sex scenes. The music in commercials has a sexual undertone. In some commercials, a half-naked woman is standing next to the car they're trying to sell. So it's no wonder that young people get involved in sex at such an early age. Our children are exposed to much more than we ever were, and much earlier in life. Their sexual drive is triggered at a far earlier age than ours was, but thank God, we can be free.

Jesus came to the earth, picked up the scroll, and preached Isaiah's sermon. Look in Luke chapter 4.

> Luke 4:18–19
> 18 The Spirit of the Lord is upon me, because he hath anointed me to preach the gospel to the poor; he hath sent me to heal the brokenhearted, to preach deliverance to the captives, and recovering of sight to the blind, to set at liberty them that are bruised,
> 19 To preach the acceptable year of the Lord.

Verse 18 says clearly that Jesus came to deliver the captives, so no matter what you're being held captive by, you can be delivered.

A Plan of Action

Here is a fourfold strategy for overcoming addictive behavior.

1. *There must be mental resolve.* First Thessalonians 4:4 says, "Every one of you should know how to possess his vessel in sanctification and honour." I need to identify where I'm weak.

2. *There must be physical restraint.* The Bible says, "Enter not into the path of the wicked, and go not in the way of evil men. Avoid it, pass not by it, turn from it, and pass away" (Prov. 4:14–15). If I know I have a weakness, then

I need to surround myself with certain protections to help me.

If a married man knows his weakness is pretty women, then he should make sure his wife is with him as much as possible. He shouldn't trust himself; he should protect himself. He shouldn't let women call him on the phone. If they want to talk, he should let his wife handle it. He has to know how to protect his vessel. The same is true for any other weakness. Every man has to know his weakness and he has to restrain himself physically in that area.

3. *There must be spiritual resistance.* James 4:7 says, "Submit yourselves therefore to God. Resist the devil, and he will flee from you." Resistance means if you find yourself in a situation where you know the devil is trying to get to you in your area of weakness, you don't give in. You resist that attack. You come against it in your mind. You don't play with thoughts about it. You don't get information about it so you can come back to it later. You resist it. It isn't anything but temptation, and being tempted is not a sin. *Yielding* to the temptation is a sin. Don't beat yourself up because you're tempted. Jesus was tempted. The Bible says He was tempted in all points like we are, yet He didn't sin (Heb. 4:15).

4. *There must be a righteous regimen.* I must set up a system in my life that keeps my body in check. For me to have a righteous regimen, my life must have structure. I must have Bible-based confessions about myself that I make daily. I must do things consistently. And I must be accountable. Every married man ought to be

accountable to his wife for how he spends his time. You can't just do whatever you want to. You're a holy man, a man of faith, a born-again man, and you ought to be accountable to your wife. She needs to know where you are. That will help you.

Breaking the Power of Sin

When the Bible talks about me resisting the devil and the power of sin being broken over my life, it means what it says. Look in First John chapter 1.

> 1 John 1:9
> 9 If we confess our sins, he is faithful and just to forgive us our sins, and to cleanse us from all unrighteousness.

According to this verse, if I confess my sin, God will forgive me and cleanse me. To break the power of sin over my life, *first I have to be honest with myself.* I have to admit that this thing has me in its grip. If you can hardly wait for everybody at home to go to sleep so you can get on the Internet, then it's got you. At one time it was hard to get pictures of naked people. Now you can get them for free in the privacy of your home. So if you've fallen into the trap, you have to be honest. You didn't mean to get tripped up. You were just curious, and it hooked you.

Second, I have to repent for sinning against God. Second Corinthians 7:10 says that godly sorrow worketh repentance. I have to understand that God can help me with this problem.

Third, I must choose to renounce the open door that I've given the devil. He didn't take place. I gave him place, and I have to renounce that.

Fourth, I have to go through the process of evicting the Satanic encroachment. I do that with the words of my mouth and the blood of Jesus, and by submitting myself to ministry. A person in this situation is not demon-possessed; he is oppressed, and that oppression can be broken. Confessing the blood of Jesus over his thought life can cleanse it. Your confession can be as simple as:

> *Father, I plead the blood of Jesus over my thought life and I cast down imaginations and every high thing that exalteth itself against the knowledge of God and bring into captivity every thought to the obedience of Christ. (Hebrews 9:13-14; 2 Corinthians 10:5.)*

Fifth, I must trust the Word of God and not my feelings. In other words, once you've renounced the open door and lordship of Satan and evicted his encroachment into your life, you're free. But your feelings have been trained another way. To retrain them, you have to consistently confess the Word of God and the blood of Jesus over your life so that your full freedom manifests and the desires of the past are erased.

King David committed murder over a woman. (See Second Samuel chapter 11.) Pornography got him into it. He saw the girl bathing and kept looking at her. He knew the time of day she would be out there. He didn't have the Internet, but he had access. He went out on his balcony and looked at her, even when it was time for him to go to war.

Then he got bold enough to ask who she was, and had sex with her, and she got pregnant.

Now, instead of going to God at that time and repenting, David thought his cover-up plan was better. He brought the woman's husband, Uriah the Hittite, home from the battle-field. But her husband wouldn't have sex with her, so David sent him back to the battlefield with a message to his commander to put him in a situation where he would be killed. David was directly responsible for Uriah's death. Then David married the girl and tried to act like everything was okay…until the prophet came (2 Sam. 12:1–14).

It could be that you've sinned and you've been masquerad-ing like everything's okay, and through what you've been reading in this book the Lord has sent the prophet to you today. But it's not a day of embarrassment for you; it's a day of freedom. God has much more for you to do in life. To do it, you can't stay trapped in the situation you're in.

You have to make a decision, like David, to repent. In Psalm 51, David cried out to God and asked for mercy, and then he said, "Purge me with hyssop" (v. 7). He knew that a cleansing had to take place. In the New Testament, in Hebrews 9:14, the Word of God sheds light on the cleansing power of the blood of Jesus.

5

A Man and
His Maintenance

In this chapter we're going to look at how to maintain our spiritual life or, in other words, what to do in order to secure our spiritual growth and maturity so we don't backslide. We'll see what we must do in order to maintain spiritual fitness. Just as an athlete has to be disciplined in his eating, in his exercise, and in his training, so the Christian man has to commit himself to a spiritual regimen that will ensure his readiness to walk in righteousness.

The Apostle Peter tells us some things to do in order to remain strong spiritually. We find them in his second letter to the church.

2 Peter 1:3-10

3 According as his divine power hath given unto us all things that pertain unto life and godliness, through the knowledge of him that hath called us to glory and virtue:

4 Whereby are given unto us exceeding great and precious promises: that by these ye might be partakers of the divine

nature, having escaped the corruption that is in the world through lust.

5 And beside this, giving all diligence, add to your faith virtue; and to virtue knowledge;

6 And to knowledge temperance; and to temperance patience; and to patience godliness;

7 And to godliness brotherly kindness; and to brotherly kindness charity.

8 For if these things be in you, and abound, they make you that ye shall neither be barren nor unfruitful in the knowledge of our Lord Jesus Christ.

9 But he that lacketh these things is blind, and cannot see afar off, and hath forgotten that he was purged from his old sins.

10 Wherefore the rather, brethren, give diligence to make your calling and election sure: for if ye do these things, ye shall never fall.

God has given us all things that pertain unto life and godliness through our knowledge of His Word. By laying hold of God's promises, we can escape the corruption that is in the world.

To cultivate our spiritual regimen, we must make three basic things part of our life. We must pray. We must meditate. And we must worship. To the degree that any man of faith will commit himself to stay built up in these areas, he will stay spiritually fit.

Do you have some sort of physical exercise program? If you do, you know that the longer you stay with that program, the more stamina you'll have to do it. Whether it's running or lifting weights, the longer you do it, the more stamina you'll have. And it's the same with spiritual things.

When you first start out, just like anything else, it's more difficult, but when you practice these things as a lifestyle, then not only do they become easier, but you start seeing tremendous results.

If you lift weights and do weight training, you know that the first day you go to the gym and pick up those weights, you can't do much. But if you stay with the eating regimen and the weight regimen and the training, before long you'll see results.

It works the same way spiritually. A lot of people want instant spiritual results, but that's not how it happens. You have to commit yourself to developing a prayer life and to disciplining yourself to meditate on the Word and to worship. If you'll do these things, you will become a spiritual champion.

Prayer

Most people are not excited about prayer. When you see prayer as some sterile conversation that you have with the air, then of course that's not exciting. But when you understand that God has given you the privilege of talking to Him yourself, without needing someone else to talk to Him for you, you'll see prayer differently. You can come to God for yourself. God wants a personal relationship with you.

If you grew up in church and heard the deacons praying those long prayers, you can almost be intimidated in your prayer life. You may think that you have to pray that way— quoting poems and putting a little music with your prayers so they'll be heard. No, God understands you when you talk to Him straight up.

The Bible clearly says that men ought to pray. We see this in Luke chapter 18.

Luke 18:1

1 And he [Jesus] spake a parable unto them to this end, that men ought always to pray, and not to faint.

Fainting means quitting. So fainting is something that can be prevented if I pray. And if a pray-er won't quit, then when a person quits, it's obvious that he hasn't been praying.

Many people don't know how to pray. They think they have to quote poems before God will hear them. They think they have to pray something like, "From everlasting to everlasting, Thou art God, through endless years the same. Lord, here I am—knee bent, body bowed—my face toward mother earth from which I've come. Thank you, Lord, that my bed was not my cooling board, and my cover was not my winding sheet. And you suffered my life to roll on just a few more years." You may say, "I can't do that." Hey, there's good news! You don't have to! In Matthew chapter 22, Jesus told some religious people that the way they saw things was wrong.

Matthew 22:29

29 Jesus answered and said unto them, Ye do err, not knowing the scriptures, nor the power of God.

We don't have to have some formula to pray, but most people fail to understand that you have to learn to pray. That's why the disciples said to Jesus, "Lord, teach us to pray" (Luke 11:1). A prayer life is learned. It doesn't happen automatically, so, Jesus taught His disciples to pray. He gave them a model prayer, and it can be our model prayer too. We call it the Lord's

Prayer, but it's basically an outline for how we can pray. Prayer is so simple. It's really you just having a conversation with God. He wants you to talk to Him, and the more you talk to Him, the more comfortable you'll be when you do it.

Developing a Spiritual Regimen

I think that developing a regimen to pray or carry out any other spiritual activity is almost like potty training. If you've had kids, you'll understand this. When you're in the potty-training stage, you have to set a time and a place. After a while, the child grows up to the point where he knows when and where to go. But before he develops to that point, you have to have a place for the pot, and you have to set a time for him to go. Even when he doesn't feel like he needs to go to the pot, you tell him, "Go sit on the pot." Nine times out of ten, while he's sitting there, something happens. In the same way, when you're learning to pray, you need to set a place and time to pray—whether it's at night, in the morning, or both. I'm not saying you have to pray for an hour, but at least you've set your time.

And when you talk to God, get real with Him. Matthew 6:8 tells us that He already knows what you have need of before you ask, so you can be open with Him and express your deepest desire and concern. In the church I pastor, we have prayer campaigns. We pray for specific things at different times. You have to begin to pray. You have to develop the discipline to do it.

The awesome thing about prayer is that you get answers. God answers prayer, and He doesn't answer it, "Yes, no, maybe, wait a while." That isn't what the Bible says. Look in Jeremiah chapter 33.

> Jeremiah 33:3
> 3 Call unto me, and I will answer thee, and show thee great and mighty things, which thou knowest not.

We see in this verse that God answers prayer. When I know how to pray, I can expect God to answer my prayer. Prayer is not a waste of time, it's an investment in my future. Here's more scripture that shows that.

> John 16:23–24
> 23 And in that day ye shall ask me nothing. Verily, verily, I say unto you, Whatsoever ye shall ask the Father in my name, he will give it you.
> 24 Hitherto have ye asked nothing in my name: ask, and ye shall receive, that your joy may be full.

We see again here that God answers prayer. When I approach prayer with the mindset that I'm not wasting my time but I'm cooperating with a spiritual principle that will yield results in my life, then prayer takes on a whole new scope. I don't have to be ashamed that I don't know how to pray like somebody else prays. I can come to God and be as real as I want to be.

All I need to understand is that God answers prayer and He hears me when I pray according to His will. Look at these verses in First John chapter 5.

> 1 John 5:14–15
> 14 And this is the confidence that we have in him, that, if we ask any thing according to his will, he heareth us:

15 And if we know that he hear us, whatsoever we ask, we know that we have the petitions that we desired of him.

So, how do I know that God hears me? I know He hears me when I pray according to His will. I do not judge the effectiveness of my prayer based on how I feel. These verses in the Bible don't mention feelings.

There are some things that can affect my prayers. According to First Peter 3:7, my relationship with my spouse can affect whether God hears my prayers. Learning that changed my life. Years ago, my wife and I were having a lot of trouble and I really didn't want to read this scripture, but I couldn't take it out of the Bible.

1 Peter 3:7

7 Likewise, ye husbands, dwell with them according to knowledge, giving honour unto the wife, as unto the weaker vessel, and as being heirs together of the grace of life; that your prayers be not hindered.

So, my prayer life can be hindered if my relationship with my spouse isn't right. That's motivation to get along.

As you develop your prayer life, you ought to get beyond just blindly reciting, "Our Father which art in heaven, Hallowed be thy name." Now, you can use that prayer as a guide. "Our Father which art in heaven, Hallowed be thy name…" is a time of worship. "Thy kingdom come. Thy will be done in earth, as it is in heaven" can be you declaring that the Kingdom of God is coming into your life, and that you are surrendering your heart, your will, and your way to Him. It can be a point of submission.

When you get to "give us this day our daily bread," you can talk to God about your needs. You can say, "Hey, God, You declared that You would supply all my needs (Phil. 4:19), and because I'm a giver, men give to me—good measure, pressed down, shaken together, and running over (Luke 6:38). I'm a tither, Father. Therefore, I believe that the windows of heaven are opened up unto me (Mal. 3:10). Doors of opportunity are opened for me. I give to the man of God. Therefore, the same grace that is on his life is on my life (Phil. 1:7). So I thank You, Father, that I go first-class in life. I eat the best, ride the best, and wear the best."

When you get to, "And forgive us our debts, as we forgive our debtors" (Matt. 6:12), you can say, "Father, in the Name of Jesus, I just thank you for forgiveness of sin. I open up my heart to you. Holy Spirit, reveal to me errors and transgressions in my life, because it's my desire to please You." And when the Spirit of God reveals those things to you, say, "Father, Your Word says that if I confess my sins, You're faithful and just to forgive me and cleanse me of all unrighteousness (1 John 1:9). Thy kingdom come. Thy will be done. Lord, I don't want to learn by trial and error. My ears are open to hear Your Word, and my heart is open to receive it. Thank You, Father. I sit under the Word of God. I learn Your Word and revelation comes to me."

As you begin to pray in these areas, you'll spend longer in each one. When you come to "Thy kingdom come, thy will be done," you can pray God's will over your family, your church, and your business. When you get to "give us this day our daily bread," you can ask God to bless your work, your business, and your daily provisions. And of course, you end your prayer the same way you started it—with praise and worship. That's how you develop a prayer life.

Meditation

Meditation is so exciting when you learn how to do it. Meditation changed my ministry and took my whole life to another level. I grew up in church and heard about meditation, but nobody ever taught me how to do it. The Lord taught me. My book *Mental Toughness for Success*² explains the revelation God gave me on this. God told me that if I would put this revelation into practice, He'd take me to heights I hadn't even imagined at that time, and He's done just that. Every Christian man needs to know how to master the process of meditation. Look in Psalm 1.

> Psalm 1:1–2
> 1 Blessed is the man that walketh not in the counsel of the ungodly, nor standeth in the way of sinners, nor sitteth in the seat of the scornful.
> 2 But his delight is in the law of the LORD; and in his law doth he meditate day and night.

God wants us to meditate day and night in His law—His Word. Now what's going to happen to the man who does this?

> Psalm 1:3
> 3 And he shall be like a tree planted by the rivers of water, that bringeth forth his fruit in his season; his leaf also shall not wither; and whatsoever he doeth shall prosper.

Meditation is your ticket out of where you are. If you can learn and master the process of meditation, it will be for you the pathway to a whole other life. Now, I've been looking forward to getting to the next scripture. Look in Joshua chapter 1.

Joshua 1:8

8 This book of the law shall not depart out of thy mouth; but thou shalt meditate therein day and night….

Notice that the Lord said the same thing here to Joshua that the writer of Psalm 1 said: he was to meditate in God's Word day and night. And why did God tell him to do that?

Joshua 1:8

…that thou mayest observe to do according to all that is written therein: for then thou shalt make thy way prosperous, and then thou shalt have good success.

So we see in the Scriptures that there's an inseparable link between meditation and success. Now I'll show this to you in the New Testament. In First Timothy chapter 4, Paul wrote to Timothy about this process of meditation.

1 Timothy 4:15

15 Meditate upon these things; give thyself wholly to them; that thy profiting may appear to all.

Paul told Timothy, "If you'll meditate, folks will see something. You'll have some results."

A Lesson on Meditation

I'm going to give you a quick lesson on meditation. To transform us, God has to work within the framework of how He created us. He has limited Himself to that. When God wants to expand our belief system, He does it through meditation. (Joshua 1:8; Psalms 2:8; Psalms 1:1.)

You believe what you believe, think what you think, and act the way you act because of four factors in your life: your environment, credible people who spoke into your life, repetitious information, and life's experiences. An experience produces the most potent impact on what you believe. It doesn't matter what happens to others, what *you* experience has more impact on you than anything else.

When a man comes to the Lord Jesus Christ, God begins to work within these four areas to transform him. Number one, He changes his environment. He says, "Come out from among them. Be separate from the world" (2 Cor. 6:17). Number two, He changes the authority over his life. He says, "From now on, I'm the greatest authority. My Word is the authority over all authorities" (Rom. 10:9; James 1:21). Number three, He requires him to do some things on a repetitious basis. And number four, as the man does these things, he will experience God in a new and refreshing way.

Remember: an experience produces the most potent impact on what a person believes. For example, suppose I introduce you to the manufacturer of a certain chair. He has the chair with him, and he has all the test data about that chair. He says the chair will hold the weight of any person. You see other people who look like they weigh more than you do come up and sit in the chair, and the chair sustains their weight. Then you get up and go sit in the chair, and the chair collapses. What will you believe about the chair? You'll believe that the chair won't hold your weight. You couldn't care less about what the data says or about what happened to others. All you know is, *your* experience was, "I sat on the chair and the chair didn't hold me." Your experience had more impact on what you believe than what others said or did.

We have three types of experiences. First, there is what I like to call a natural experience. It's something I actually live through. Second, there is a soulish experience. This takes place only in the arena of my mind. For instance, have you ever had a dream that was so real, you thought you were there? Maybe you thought somebody was chasing you, and right before they caught you, you woke up. You were sweating and your heart was beating fast, yet you had not left your bed. It all happened in your mind, yet it seemed real to you because your belief system cannot distinguish between the various types of experiences. It cannot tell whether an experience is real, or soulish, or the third kind of experience we're going to look at—a *spiritual* experience.

A Spiritual Experience

A spiritual experience is one that God initiates, or allows you to initiate, so that you see on the canvas of your imagination the end result of what God has promised. Whenever God wanted to transform a man's belief system in an accelerated fashion, He gave him a vision or a dream. Visions and dreams are spiritual experiences.

Maybe you grew up hearing about Ezekiel and the valley of dry bones (see Ezekiel chapter 37). Ezekiel was never physically there. He saw that valley in a vision. God gave Ezekiel that vision to transform his belief system so that God could get him to believe that he could bring his fragmented nation back together.

Whenever God wanted to transform a man's belief system, He would give him a spiritual experience, because an experience makes the most potent impact on what a man believes. A spiritual experience can seem so real to a person's belief system that he actually thinks he is living through it. When Ezekiel came out of this vision, God instructed him and said, "Now, you go and preach unity to My people." Because Ezekiel had had this spiritual experience, he was ready to go.

Meditation is a spiritual experience that God allows man to initiate, so that man himself can work at transforming his belief system. To meditate means to engage in mental exercise; focus one's thoughts; to plan or project in the mind.[3]

There are several aspects of meditation. Let's start by looking at these three: *verbalization, visualization,* and *internalization.* First, let's consider verbalization.

Verbalization is the foundational component of the meditation process. The desire of your heart during this process must be based on the Word of God. God told Joshua to meditate in His Word day and night (Joshua 1:8). The psalmist said the same thing in Psalm 1:2. When we verbalize, we create images of our future on the canvas of our imaginations. Secondly, we speak faith filled words into the situation and it triggers divine assistance. Visualization is being able to see or envision the object of my meditation, which is the end result of what the Word of God promises. If the Word of God says He restores me to health, then I see myself healthy again. If the

Word of God says that I'm wealthy, I see myself wealthy. I see myself enjoying my new car. If the Word of God says that I'm blessed in my relationships, I see myself having a good conversation with my wife. As I do these things, I will internalize what the Holy Spirit is showing me.

The Components of an Experience

Any experience has several components: words, images, and emotions. In meditation, I have words, because I have the Word of God. I have images, because I see the end result of what I'm believing for on the canvas of my imagination. And I have emotions. The Bible tells me to set my affection on things above (Col. 3:2). *Affection* is emotion. Through praise I internalize what I'm seeing. So, I have the components of an experience: words, images, and emotions.

The entire advertising industry is based on this principle. Advertising people know that if they show you a product along with something that you're emotionally attached to, and they show it to you repeatedly, it will change what you believe. So they get an actor or an athlete—somebody you like—and they let him hold the product. Because he has the product, you associate the same feelings you have toward him with the product. That television commercial has three components: words, images, and emotions. The advertising people play that commercial day and night, repetitiously, because you have been designed so that what you hear repeatedly affects your belief system.

Meditation is your personal, customized, Holy Ghost commercial. You allow the Word of God to formulate it. The Holy Spirit paints it on the canvas of your imagination, and you look at it repeatedly until it transforms what you believe.

All visualization has to have a reference. If I told you to go outside and find a Cadillac, you'd have to know what a Cadillac was. Knowledge is based on knowledge, so, you may need a point of reference to help you understand what God is saying in His Word.

God told Abraham, who was already old and had no children, that his own son would be his heir and that he would have many descendants. Abraham couldn't understand that, so God took him outside his tent at night and told him to count the stars, if he could. Then God said, "so shall thy seed be" (Gen. 15:5). God was saying to him, "Hey, look at the stars and imagine the face of a child on every star." He was giving him a reference point.

God told Joshua, "As I was with Moses, so shall I be with you" (Josh. 1:5). In other words, God was telling him to imagine himself doing what he had seen Moses do. And Joshua was Moses' right-hand man. He had seen Moses do a lot.

All visualization has to have a point of reference. If I begin to see myself as successful with a contemporary reference point as the Word of God says (Josh. 1:8), and I keep meditating on that day and night, over and over, it will transform my belief system.

This is a powerful principle. When the Lord showed this to me, my office was a five- by five-foot closet. I used to go to First Baptist Church, which was at that time, the largest church in

Houston. God told me to go there and sit in that auditorium that seated three thousand people and imagine myself preaching on that stage. He told me to imagine the place filled with people and me walking up and down the stage preaching. Today, I don't have to imagine. I have a successful ministry and I preach to thousands each week.

Jacob's Life Transformed

In Genesis 30:28–43, we see how God worked with Jacob to transform his whole life through this same principle of meditation. God had a covenant with Jacob, and He was going to bless him, but He had to have Jacob's participation.

Jacob's father-in-law, Laban, had tricked him into working for him for a number of years. Then God gave Jacob a creative idea. So Jacob went to Laban and said, "I don't want to work on salary any longer. I want to work on commission." What was Jacob's commission? He asked Laban for all the speckled, spotted, and brown sheep and goats that Laban's herd would produce.

Laban, who was a trickster, thought, *Now, solid-colored animals mating together produce solid-colored offspring, and speckled and spotted animals produce speckled and spotted offspring. I'm going to take advantage of this chump.* So he said to Jacob, "You're a real smart guy. We'll do that." Then Laban had his sons take all the speckled, spotted, and brown animals out of his herd and move them a three-days' journey away from Jacob. That left Jacob with only Laban's solid-colored animals.

Well, how was Jacob going to get any animals that belonged to him? God told Jacob to get some tree limbs and peel the bark off in spots until they resembled the hide of the animals he wanted. Then God told him to set the limbs by the watering troughs where the animals mated. When offspring were born, they were speckled and spotted.

Jacob said later that an angel told him, "You sit there and you look and imagine that the animals being produced will be spotted and speckled" (Gen. 31:10–12). The genetic miracle did not take place because of what the animals saw, but because of what Jacob saw.

If Jacob had had a camera, he wouldn't have had to peel back the bark of the tree limbs and set them there. All he would have needed was a picture of what he wanted. Today, we don't have to peel back the bark on tree limbs.

When you are believing for something, you need a picture of it. The meditation process can be accelerated with what I call a visual booster. Now, remember this statement: *where there's clarity of vision, there is acceleration toward a known goal.* Have you ever been driving and you drove into fog? You knew where you were going, but because of the fog you couldn't see. You had to slow down. When the fog lifted, you accelerated, because where there is clarity of vision, there is acceleration toward a known goal. Meditation allows you to see where you are going before you get there. Once you see yourself at your destination, you will believe you can get there.

I taught this principle years ago, and a young man who wanted to play for the Harlem Globetrotters was in the meeting. His agent had told him he would never be a

Globetrotter. He heard me talk about meditation, visualization, and internalization, and he decided he would do it. He got a picture of a Globetrotter, cut out the guy's face, put his face on there, and brought the picture to me. He said, "Pastor, I believe I'll be a Globetrotter one day. This is my booster for meditation." I saw that he'd gotten hold of what I'd said, and I told him, "Oh yeah, you got it! You got it!" Today, this fellow has been a Globetrotter for more than thirteen years. In fact, he's one of the lead players.

After the Lord taught me this principle, I taught it to everybody I could, because I knew it would expand people's faith. Years ago, one of my associate pastors got hold of it. He wanted to be a traveling minister. After service, he'd get a briefcase and ask somebody to take him to the airport. He'd get out of the car, wave at the people, and say, "I'm going to preach the gospel to the world." (He didn't get on a plane. He wasn't stupid.) Today he's preached all over the world.

You have to develop the discipline to meditate. Before I do anything, I meditate on it. People wonder how I come up with ideas. I spend time seeing myself in my future. In the early days of my ministry, I used to tell people, "I'm escaping the pain of my present by visiting my future on the canvas of my imagination." When you do that, something happens. You start believing you can do it. You start believing you can have that car or that house. You start believing you can have a better relationship or a great church. The Bible says, "If thou canst believe, all things are possible to him that believeth" (Mark 9:23).

Before I ever bought a Rolls Royce, I had pictures of one. That may not be the car you want. That's fine. Drive what you want to drive. But I wanted to drive a Rolls. So I got pictures of Rolls Royces and put them everywhere. I saw myself in a Rolls. I didn't have any money. I was broke. But I knew I wasn't going to be broke for long.

I'm trying to tell you that wherever you are in life, you can move from there. Your faith will do it. This is a spiritual exercise you can do that will help your faith. What do you have to lose? Do you have any dreams or desires? You have to see yourself there. Many times, you have to use some boosters to help. You need to see yourself in those situations.

Worship

As we said at the beginning of this chapter, three things must be part of our spiritual regimen for us to secure our spiritual growth and maturity. The first is prayer. The second is meditation. The third, which we'll look at now, is worship. The Bible says, "God is a Spirit: and they that worship him must worship him in spirit and in truth" (John 4:24). You can tie your worship in with your meditation. Do you remember that we looked at internalization? Internalization is the process by which I set my affection, or my emotions, on something. I can do that with worship. Worshipping God is an exchange. Praise brings me into His presence. But what I do once I'm there is called worship. That's when I want to talk to Him.

To worship God, I use my mind, my mouth, my mannerisms, and my money. A man has to learn to worship. God is looking for people who will worship Him—men who are not ashamed to say, "I have a relationship with God and I don't care who knows about it." Men are more free in talking about which sports team they're for than they are in telling people that they have a relationship with the Lord. Men don't mind people knowing that they're for the Cowboys or the Giants or the Rams. But you have to be free when it comes to worshipping God. "They that worship Him must worship Him in spirit and in truth."

So, I have to be a worshipper. When I worship God, I intensify His reality in my life. I invoke His power for my deliverance. I'm infused with fulfillment and joy. And I'm instructed in how to live, because not only do I talk to God; God talks to me. When I'm worshipping God, I'm going through an image transformation. I cannot be before the face of God and remain the same. We see that in this verse in Second Corinthians.

2 Corinthians 3:18
18 But we all, with open face beholding as in a glass the glory of the Lord, are changed into the same image from glory to glory, even as by the Spirit of the Lord.

The Apostle Paul said here, "As I behold His glory, I'm transformed into His image."

So as a man, I do some things for physical exercise, but I also must do some things for spiritual exercise. I must learn to pray. I must learn to meditate. And I must learn to worship. To be successful beyond what he can even imagine, every man must master these three things.

6

A Man and
His Mistakes

In this chapter we're going to look at how to recover after making a mistake. We'll do that first by looking at the story of the Prodigal Son in Luke chapter 15. You are probably familiar with this story. A young man receives his inheritance from his father, and then goes off and wastes it and ends up working in a hog pen. Let's pick up the story in verse 17.

> Luke 15:17–24
>
> 17 And when he came to himself, he said, How many hired servants of my father's have bread enough and to spare, and I perish with hunger!
>
> 18 I will arise and go to my father, and will say unto him, Father, I have sinned against heaven, and before thee,
>
> 19 And am no more worthy to be called thy son: make me as one of thy hired servants.
>
> 20 And he arose, and came to his father. But when he was yet a great way off, his father saw him, and had compassion, and ran, and fell on his neck, and kissed him.

21 And the son said unto him, Father, I have sinned against heaven, and in thy sight, and am no more worthy to be called thy son.

22 But the father said to his servants, Bring forth the best robe, and put it on him; and put a ring on his hand, and shoes on his feet:

23 And bring hither the fatted calf, and kill it; and let us eat, and be merry:

24 For this my son was dead, and is alive again; he was lost, and is found. And they began to be merry.

In this chapter, we're going to look at the maturity in manhood necessary to face and recover from mistakes. We'll also see God's commitment to help you recover from any mistake that you've made. It's about making a comeback. It's about the spiritual process involved in restoring you back to or beyond a position, posture, or privilege that you lost because of adversity.

A man needs to know how to handle mistakes. All of us make mistakes. We don't intend to. And here I'm talking about a mistake, not necessarily some sin. I'm talking about just a mistake in judgment that cost you, such as not handling business right.

For example, one time a friend gave me a stock tip, and I didn't go through the normal process I use to evaluate such tips. I got greedy and bought about fifty thousand dollars worth of that stock. And yes indeed, that baby started falling Monday and it kept on going down. I was on the phone with my broker saying, "Sell it! Sell it! Sell it!" By the time I got it sold, I had lost twenty-five grand. That was a mistake.

Then I had to tell my wife that I'd just blown twenty-five thousand dollars. Twenty-five grand. Bam! It was gone. I knew I'd gotten greedy. When I got the tip, I called my broker and told him, "As soon as the market opens, get me fifty grand of this."

He said, "Now, wait a minute. Have you checked it out?"

"Naw, naw. I know what I'm doing. Get me fifty grand."

He tried to talk me out of it. Then he called me around noon and said, "It's falling. But sometimes they turn up."

Five minutes later, he called me again. "It's still falling." Thirty minutes later… "It's still falling."

"Sell," I said.

"I'm trying."

Nobody likes to buy stock when it's falling, especially when it's taking that big of a dive. And that baby started diving quickly. It had risen fast Thursday and Friday, and the guy had given me the tip Friday, so I couldn't wait till Monday when I could buy it. Then after I lost the twenty-five thousand, I had to go talk to my wife. Now look at this verse in First John.

1 John 5:4
4 For whatsoever is born of God overcometh the world: and this is the victory that overcometh the world, even our faith.

So this is how you make a comeback after you've made a mistake. If you can't handle mistakes, you'll never be success-ful at the level God wants to take you to. You travel through the valley of mistakes on the way to success. The key is, don't stay in the valley after you make a mistake. You're going to make mistakes, but don't let a mistake turn *you* into a mistake.

You have to know how to move past mistakes in judgment. I made a mistake with money, and I had to learn how to bounce back. That's the key to success.

Mistakes can be costly. They can have devastating consequences and pull you away from the plan of God for your life. My wife and I could have started fussing and fighting, but that wouldn't have brought back the twenty-five thousand dollars. I've seen men who made mistakes and then became mean with everybody else. No, when I told my wife about the mistake, I started out by telling her what a good boy I'd been before then. I reminded her that I'd made some good investments. Then I said, "Let's go eat." And we talked about it.

You have to not let your mistakes ruin your day. The game isn't over just because your shot got blocked. You'll get the ball again. And folks will forget that your shot was blocked. It isn't over just because you failed academically. Keeping the right mental attitude is so important when you've made a blunder. You may have been terminated from your job. Well, just make sure you don't let that happen again. I know men who quit and then had second thoughts. They let somebody push them into quitting, and they told their boss what he could do with that job. But that didn't hurt the boss. He still had cash flow.

You need to know that you can recover from any mistake you've made with time and God's help. Recovery is the main thing. As I said, I'm intentionally steering away from talking about sins here. I'm talking about missed opportunities, mistakes in judgment, and similar things. Mistakes in judgment can attack your self-esteem.

A number of things can undermine your efforts to recover from a mistake. First, you can be deceived into thinking that you have to cover up your mistake. Normally, you start lying to try to do that, and that is what puts you outside of the plan of God. When that lie is exposed, you've lost credibility with those who trusted you. And trust can be a hard thing to earn. You can lose it in a moment and it may take a lifetime to rebuild. The key is, never try to cover a mistake. Be willing to own up to it. That's what a real man does.

Years ago as a pastor, I was trying to build a building. I really thought I'd heard from God. I had members investing money and backing the project. We had bought some land and hired an architect. But it was hard to get it going, and I went to God one day and asked, "What's wrong? This is hard." Then God spoke to me and said, "Son, I never told you to do that."

"I thought you did," I said. "I've even told the church folks that it was You. What am I going to do?"

"You're going to tell them you missed it," He said.

Well, that isn't good. I didn't really want to do that. But I'm glad I did. I stood up one Sunday and just told everybody, "Pastor missed it. I know you spent a lot of money and we invested a lot of money in this. I thought I'd heard from God, but I hadn't. God didn't tell me to do this, so we're going to release our faith that we can sell the land and recoup our money (because the land had depreciated), and then we'll move on."

It was quiet. Then one person started clapping, and everybody else started clapping. They stood up and we all started crying. I felt really good then. We'd blown a whole lot of money, but I was a man and stood up and faced it.

My family has confidence in me that I'll always be truthful with them. I don't ever intend to miss it. But if I do, I'm not going to cover it up with some lie. I'm not going to be Mister Untouchable where I cannot be confronted, because I'm a man. When I believe that there is a plan for fulfillment other than truth, I've been deceived.

The second thing that causes men to abandon what I call a comeback mentality and not recover from their mistakes is, they get discouraged at the persecution that living with purpose brings. In other words, it can seem easy for the moment to lie and try to get out of something. But when I choose to be a man and live by purpose and tell the truth, some people will say, "You're stupid." That's persecution. You have to understand that doing things the right way is best.

Third, you can be deceived into thinking that God's recovery plan, which includes repentance, will hurt your reputation. You can have the thought, *What are they going to think about me the next time I propose something? What will my wife think about me the next time I want to buy some stock?*

Maybe you can relate to this example. Suppose you bought a car and you thought it was a good deal, but it turned out to be a lemon. And before you bought it, your wife told you, "We don't need that car." But you said, "Naw, naw, it's a good car," because you liked the sunroof. That's all you liked about it. You bought the car from one of those "tote your note" lots because it had a hole in the top and it was your dream to have a car where you could look up and see the sky. Never mind the number of miles on it or what the man was asking for it. He told you a little bit down, and a little bit every week.

Or maybe you made a business deal that you thought was going to be great. You told your wife, "This is going to be our ticket out," and it ended up being somebody else's ticket that you paid for.

The fourth thing that can hurt a man's comeback is, he can get discouraged and disappointed at the lack of promised participation from others. In other words, there are times when you believe others can help you, but the people who you think are supposed to help you may not be the ones who actually help. If your focus is on God, you'll never be disappointed.

The fifth thing that can interfere with you having a comeback mentality is a decline in your spiritual devotion. When you're not as spiritually in tune as you want to be, your diligence will be diminished. The Bible says that men ought always to pray and not faint (Luke 18:1). If we're not praying, we're subject to fainting, or quitting.

The sixth thing that can undermine your comeback from a mistake is if you've disguised your mistake with what you believe is an unbeatable cover-up plan and fabricated a lie, and that has pacified you.

The Laws of Spiritual Recovery

So, what do I have to do in order to recover spiritually from a mistake? There are four laws that I must respect. First, there is *the law of environment.* The law of environment says, there is a specific sphere of exposure and influence that I'm subject to, and it's going to exert influence on me. The people I'm around are going to affect me positively or negatively, so I have to make sure I'm around the right people.

Your environment will change you before you change it. Your environment will cause you to blossom, or it will cause you to be barren. Your environment—the people you're around—is a silent, prophetic declaration that speaks of your future. If you want to see your future, look at the guys you hang around with. Take a moment and think about them. Are they broke? Are they working? Are they committing adultery and fornication? Are these the kind of guys you're hanging with? Then that's your future. Your environment will change you before you change it. If you hang around guys who have unhappy marriages, then you're going to start finding fault with your wife too. So, I have to make some environmental changes. I have to know who I need to hang around.

Let me give you some guidelines about people that you need to spend time with who will be a support network for you in the midst of mistakes. Number one, you need to hang around people who live according to purpose. In other words, you need to hang around people who understand that we've been created to worship God and serve Him.

Number two, you need to have people in your sphere of influence who are productive—people who have something and are going somewhere.

Number three, you need to be around people who think progressively—people who can stimulate your thinking.

If you're a single man and you're looking for a wife, don't just look for something easy. Being married is more than having a body next to you in bed. You need a woman who will stimulate your mind. Don't just get some old, easy woman. You'll get tired of her after you marry her. Now, a thinking woman may make a demand on you. You can't fool her. You can't flash some dollars at her and have her say, "Oooh, you're so handsome!" when you know you're ugly. You want a woman who can stimulate your thinking. Don't be intimidated by a strong woman.

Number four, you need to be around people who live by principle. We looked at living by principle earlier in this book.

Number five, you need to be around people who can control their passions. You need to spend time with other men who can control their flesh and resist temptation.

Number six, you need to be around men who promote others. You don't need to spend time with jealous men. They are dangerous to be around. The Bible says, "Let nothing be done through strife or vainglory; but in lowliness of mind let each esteem other better than themselves. Look not every man on his own things, but every man also on the things of others" (Phil. 2:3–4). Men who live like that are the ones you need to be around. They'll be happy when you succeed; they won't compete with you. Some men will talk you out of doing something they plan to do. They'll tell you not to do it, and then they'll go and do it.

Psalm 1 has something to say about a man's environment.

Psalm 1:1

1 Blessed is the man that walketh not in the counsel of the ungodly, nor standeth in the way of sinners, nor sitteth in the seat of the scornful.

To be able to recover from mistakes, I need to make sure I'm in the right environment. I need to be in a bounce-back environment. When I lost that twenty-five thousand dollars on that stock deal, I had a wife who understood. That's a lot of money to blow in one day, but she knew who she was married to, and that he was going to work and make that up. And I had other support groups around me. I made the mistake because I got greedy and didn't do my homework, and I suffered the consequences. But I wasn't around people who were putting their foot on me. I was around people who understood the process of success.

The Law of Expectation

Next, to recover from a mistake, I need to respect the law of expectation. Look in Hebrews chapter 11.

Hebrews 11:1

1 Now faith is the substance of things hoped for, the evidence of things not seen.

Hoped for in this verse means "expected." Expectation says, "The anticipation of some future event affects my passion, my perspective, and ultimately, my pursuits." In other words, my anticipation affects my attitude.

My expectations are not blind. The Bible says, "In the mouth of two or three witnesses, shall every word be established" (Matt. 18:16; 2 Cor. 13:1). I have a chart that lists several criteria. I establish a justifiable expectation when it lines up with at least two of the things on my list. The things I expect and pursue are based on these criteria:

A justifiable expectation must be based on a promise from a reliable source.

A justifiable expectation must be based on the proven—the unchangeable and indiscriminate principles and laws of success.

A justifiable expectation must be based on the previous—on experience with similar factors or variables.

A justifiable expectation must be based on the personal. This is an expectation based on a reliable testimony from a trustworthy individual.

A justifiable expectation must be based on the prophetic. That is, it must be based on the Word of God for my time and my generation.

When any two of those elements line up, then I have a justifiable expectation. I only expect those things that line up with these factors.

An Example

Suppose someone tells me, "I'm going give you a million dollars." If that statement doesn't line up with at least two of these factors, I'm not going to expect that. I'll shake his hand and say, "Well, praise the Lord." But I won't expect it.

But suppose the statement lines up? The first criterion for a justifiable expectation is that it must be based on a promise from a reliable source. If Bill Gates said it, I know he has the money, so it's met the first criterion. If some folks I know said it who have the money and keep their word when they give it, then I have a justifiable expectation that I'm going to see that million dollars. That statement first is a promise from a reliable source, and second is from a trustworthy individual. These people I know have good track records.

So, a justifiable expectation is not based on just one of these factors; it's based on at least two of them. "In the mouths of two or three witnesses, shall every word be established."

The law of expectations will help you control the "oopses" in your life. An "oops" is when you make a mistake and then you think about it later and say, "Oops." That has happened to a lot of people in relation to multilevel marketing. There's nothing wrong with multilevel marketing, but a person has to work at it. Don't let somebody sell you on a pipe dream. You can't justifiably expect to sign a piece of paper one day and give somebody twenty-five dollars, and then make a million dollars a month. It isn't going to happen like that.

The Law of Expression

To recover from a mistake, I must respect the law of environment and surround myself with the right people, and I must respect the law of expectation and make sure my expectations are justifiable. Then, I must respect the law of expression.

The law of expression says, "One's position in faith, and one's strength of faith, is not determined by a revelation. It is measured by corresponding action in agreement with that revelation." The law of expression has to do with what I do. I must understand that faith is not sitting around twiddling my thumbs. An overemphasis on knowledge and revelation often robs believers of the faith action necessary to trigger the supernatural power of God.

I've seen people who say they're in faith, and they're doing nothing. Faith has to do with me *making a declaration* in agreement with God's Word; *having a demonstration,* or acting on what I believe; *having determination* to hold to the course I'm on until I see the results of my faith; and *having a dedication* to God through it all. So, if I'm in faith, I'm going to be working. I'm going to be doing something. Don't tell me you're in faith for a job and all you're doing is sitting at home watching TV. If that's all you're doing, you're not in faith.

The Law of Endurance

The law of endurance has to do with the discipline and resolve that I have to overcome hardships. The law of endurance says, "When a believer functions righteously according to proven principles of faith, and he holds to the faith course uncompromisingly, he will overcome obstacles, hardships, and harassments to obtain the object of his faith." Look in Hebrews chapter 10.

Hebrews 10:35–36

35 Cast not away therefore your confidence, which hath great recompence of reward.

36 For ye have need of patience, that, after ye have done the
will of God, ye might receive the promise.

I must be willing to hold fast to my confession of faith. I
must be willing to fight for it. That means I must be willing to
overcome some barriers. To the degree that I'm willing to do
that and activate this law of endurance, I'll see results in my
life. My mistakes will not be fatal—to my finances, to my
family relationships, or to any other area of my life.

Now, let's look at some of the kinds of mistakes we make.
Sometimes we make mistakes because we think we're right
and we're really wrong. For example, in relationships, we may
think we're right, and we're wrong. When we realize we're
wrong, what do we do? Well, if we're men, we own up to the fact
that we missed it. But I have to understand that when I make a
mistake, it's not the end of the world. The best of us blow it.

The Process of Recovery

The story of the Prodigal Son found in Luke 15:11–24 offers
a good illustration of the steps involved in the process of
recovering from mistakes. First, the younger son *came to
himself.* He said, "Man, I have messed up." He was honest
about his fallen state. When you make a mistake, the thing to
do to recover from it is not to try to cover it up.

Then the Prodigal Son *said to himself.* In other words, he
expressed his conviction and he repented. Then *he settled
himself.* He understood the discomfort that he might have to
experience in the process of recovery. He said, "I'm going
home. I'll just be a servant. If my mistake has caused me to

lose all privileges, and all I'll be able to do is serve and live in the servants' house, so be it. It's better than being out here by myself."

The next thing the Prodigal Son did was, *he presented himself.* In other words, he followed through with his repentance. Don't just think it. Do it. Have you ever thought about asking forgiveness from your spouse or family for something, and you never did it? If so, don't let that happen again. Be a man and follow through with it.

Next, the Prodigal Son *humbled himself.* He positioned himself under protective authority. In other words, he went to his father and said, "Okay, Father, I'm getting right back in place." When you hold up the truth, you get right back under the Father's protection, and you can experience His benefits.

Next, the Prodigal Son *trusted the process.* He depended upon someone higher than himself to help him. And to recover from our mistakes, that's Who we have to depend on. When we make a mistake, we don't cover it up. We admit it. We quit it. We come clean, and then we trust the process of repentance. Repentance puts us back in line, but not at the back of the line.

Then, the Prodigal Son *experienced the comeback.* His father accepted him and restored him.

We have to deal with our mistakes, because we're going to make them, especially if we have a desire to succeed. The devil will put stumbling-blocks and barriers in our way, but we'll overcome them. It's a fight we'll win.

Don't let a mistake cause you to be a mistake. Remember: the road to success passes through the valley of mistakes. But don't stay there.

7

A Man and
His Mentor

In this chapter we'll deal with a man and his mentor, or a man and his mentors. You can have more than one. It's the order of God to teach us and train us by example. We see this in Hebrews chapter 6.

Hebrews 6:12

12 That ye be not slothful, but followers of them who through faith and patience inherit the promises.

The word *followers* here is a translation of a Greek word that means "to imitate." (The New Testament was written in Greek.) The Bible tells us that we are to imitate certain others. When we understand that that's the order of God—that's the way He set things up—then we don't need to be concerned about losing our true identity by imitating how others perform principles. We don't imitate a person's personality; we imitate how they activate and work principles in their lives.

We see this mentoring process throughout the Bible. Every man needs to know how to find his mentor, and how to glean from his mentor without interrupting his mentor's assignment. You probably admire your mentor because things are working for him. The last thing you want to do is be a distraction to your mentor.

God's plan is that we learn from others who are successful. Throughout the Bible, we see that each of us has a responsibility not only to learn from others but also to teach others. God wants us to be fruitful. Look in Genesis chapter 1.

Genesis 1:28

28 And God blessed them, and God said unto them, Be fruitful, and multiply....

To be fruitful and multiply is to reproduce after your own kind. This is not limited to you reproducing yourself biologically. You should be reproducing yourself after your own kind spiritually and in ministry as well.

First of all, you need to find a mentor and learn how to glean from that mentor. I have this saying: "He who aggressively seeks a mentor is himself a mentor in the making," because when you understand God's plan, you're not going to be a shoplifter. In other words, you're not going to learn from somebody and then not pass what you've learned on to others. The New Testament Church is built upon this principle of men teaching men.

So, what is a mentor? A mentor is an experienced teacher, counselor, and role model who is willing to directly or indirectly impart what he or she knows into the lives of willing others. We're all the sum total of what others have poured into our lives that we have chosen to make a part of our lives. When we look at our lives, we see some things that we've learned from somebody else.

I'm writing a book about all of the things that I've learned from my various mentors, starting with my father. He was my first mentor. He didn't know he was mentoring me, but I learned so much from him. The most valuable lesson he taught me was the work ethic. My father was a good worker, so, I have problems with lazy people, because to me, that's a major dysfunction. I don't understand that. I didn't grow up seeing a man not working. That's part of the fabric that makes up my life. All things being equal, if you are able to work, you ought to be working.

As we said earlier, the Greek word translated *followers* in Hebrews 6:12 means "imitators." That's God's order—His way of doing things. I got a lot of flak early in my ministry because I used Dr. Fred Price as my model. I imitated how he activated God's principles in his life. I followed him from afar. I never wanted to get up close to him. I'd go to his crusades and sit way in the back, but I was following him. I read his books and listened to his tapes. People said, "You're just trying to be like Fred Price." I said, "That's right." I wouldn't back down, because I understood this principle of mentoring. The principle is, "Imitate those who through faith and patience have inherited the promises."

When I look for a mentor, I'm looking for someone who has what I want. I'm not looking for somebody who doesn't have it together. Criticism from my peers didn't bother me, because they were not my mentors. Look in Second Timothy chapter 2.

> 2 Timothy 2:2
>
> 2 And the things that thou hast heard of me among many witnesses, the same commit thou to faithful men, who shall be able to teach others also.

In that verse, underline "the same." That's the premise our ministry's built on. What happens in Houston in the church I pastor happens in other cities in churches pastored by men who've learned from me. I've taught other men, and they teach the same thing where they are.

Imitate Principles, Not Personality

We imitate the application of principles in our mentor's life, not his personality. We observe him from afar. And if it's the will of God for a close relationship to come to pass, God will cause it to come to pass. Never be ashamed of the mentoring process, because that is God's order—His method of doing things. I never was ashamed when people said I was trying to be like Fred Price. The man had folks standing in line to get into his church. They said, "You're going to die a copy." No I wasn't. I wasn't going to lose my identity. I am who I am. I wasn't telling people, "I'm Fred Price." I didn't change my name. Now I want you to look at this verse in Romans chapter 15.

> Romans 15:4
>
> 4 For whatsoever things were written aforetime were written for our learning, that we through patience and comfort of the scriptures might have hope.

In other words, the scriptural text is written so I can draw truths from it. And one truth I see is this mentoring process.

Mentoring is God's plan to pass on to others knowledge and wisdom to advance His Kingdom in the earth. It's not God's plan for man to get knowledge and wisdom and keep it all to himself. When I was getting ready to build a church building, I traveled around and talked to other pastors who had built buildings. Those guys didn't want to share anything with me. It amazed me that they would not share the "how-to's." One pastor I asked just gave me a tour of the building. I didn't need a tour of the building. I could see the building. I wanted to know the process he went through to build it. But none of the pastors I talked to would tell me. I promised God, "If you'll show me how to do it, I'll show everybody else."

A Mentor in the Shadows

For every man who is great in what he's doing, there is a mentor in the shadows. For every Samuel, there's an Eli. For every Peter, there's a Jesus. For every Paul, there's a Barnabas. For every Elisha, there's an Elijah. For every Joshua, there's a Moses. For every Timothy, there's a Paul. For every Hilliard, there's a Fred Price. That's just the order of God. So, we simply follow God's order. And to flow with God's order, I must know that it's okay for me to learn from others.

In the early days of my ministry I went to see Dr. Price because God had impressed upon me that he was to mentor me. It was supernatural how I got an appointment with him so quickly. As we talked, he asked me to send him one of my teaching lessons. So I sent him my best lesson. After a while he called me and said, "Young man, can you take straight talk?"

I thought he was getting ready to invite me to come preach. I thought highly of what I was doing. So I said, "Yes, sir."

"If we're going to have a relationship, you have to be able to take it straight, because I don't have time to play."

"Okay, fine."

Then he said, "Now, this tape you sent me. Tell me you're not putting this on TV."

"Doctor Price, that's a TV program."

"We have a problem," he said.

Then he just tore into it. He tore up everything—how it was edited, how the church looked, and every other part of it. Then I had a choice. I could try to defend myself, or I could understand that this man was trying to help me. He was not trying to hurt me. He could have patronized me and just said, "It looks all right," and my program would have continued to look the way it did.

Then he told me, "Young man, you are not teaching the Word." You could have told me anything else, but not that. I thought I was a hot shot. He said, "Now, you're *talking about* the Word, but you're not teaching it." So I asked him what the difference was. He said, "It's one thing to tell a man that Dallas, Texas, exists. It's another thing to tell a man how to get from Houston to Dallas. The difference between talking about the Word and teaching the Word is, in teaching the Word, you don't just tell a man what the promise of God is. You tell him how to get from where he is to where the promise is. That's the difference. There's a fine line there. You'll have folks shouting over just hearing about Dallas. But the man who'll make it in life is the one who knows how to get from where he is to where God wants him to be."

So, I told him, "Well Doctor Price, since you know how to teach the Word and I don't, I'm going to teach your lessons until I learn how to do it." Now, a lot of people say that God ought to give you your own lessons. But if you're preaching out of the Bible, you're already preaching somebody else's lesson. The Bible is somebody else's revelation from God. If you're preaching from it, you're jumping off from what they gave you. When Jesus preached His first sermon (see Luke 4:16–21), He preached Isaiah's sermon. Jesus set the example. There's no sense in reinventing the wheel. So I preached Doctor Price's sermons. I'd sit and listen to them all week long and make my outline, and then on Sunday, "Little Fred" was in the house. And I was getting results.

My church members knew what I was doing. No one who knows me will ever be able to say that I don't give my mentor credit. There's never been a platform God has given me where I did not acknowledge my mentor, even if he wasn't around, because I'm never greater than he is. What I've accomplished, I owe to him. My mentor is in my heart.

So, I must clearly understand that mentoring is God's order. I want a mentor who's not going to patronize me and just tell me nice things to keep me around. That's what I really liked about Dr. Price. When he had to be tough and hard with me, he was. I knew he loved me. And I knew that, because he wanted the best for me, he wasn't going to shortchange me. As I tell my sons and the men I mentor, "If I'm your father in ministry when I'm telling you something you want to hear, I'm also your father in ministry when I'm telling you something you *don't* want to hear."

So a mentor, if you'll let him, will correct deep dysfunctions and misguided manhood vices, because behind every dysfunction is a history of disorder, dishonor, and damage. A mentor can help you if you'll let him. If you'll allow him to talk straight to you and not take it as a personal attack, then he can help you. All this depends on your getting an up-close relationship with your mentor. A lot of folks can't handle up-close relationships. If God brings you into a close relationship with your mentor, you always have to make sure that you keep in perspective what's going on. Look at this verse in John chapter 13.

John 13:16

16 Verily, verily, I say unto you, The servant is not greater than his lord....

I'm never my mentor's equal. This is true even of mentors I had before I met Dr. Price. One of them is C. L. Jackson in Houston. Whenever I'm around him, I'm still the protégé. I'll still carry his bag. I still honor him, because I'll never be greater than him. That's how I keep my heart right. It doesn't matter if my church has more members than his, or if I have a jet and he doesn't. It's not about that. It's about the revelation from the Scriptures. The Bible says, "The student is never greater than the teacher."

Characteristics of a Mentor

As we review these characteristics of a mentor, remember, he who seeks a mentor is a mentor in the making. He needs to have the mentality that just as he is looking up to someone, there is someone else looking up to him.

- A mentor desires to impart what he knows.

- A mentor must have a good self-image.

- A mentor must be transparent and live a principle-driven life. If you live a principle-driven life, you never have to backtrack. I tell people, "If you go back twenty-two years, you'll see that I was doing the same thing I'm doing now. And if you look at me twenty years in the future, I'll be doing the same thing I'm doing now, because I'm principle-driven." I don't mind talking about my mistakes and my life. My life is transparent, because I want you to learn.

- A mentor must possess a quality or virtue worth pursuing. You have to ask yourself, "Is my life worth somebody else patterning his life after?"

- A mentor should not rob you of the life experiences that helped produce the character trait or discipline that you admire in him.

I have a lot of sons in ministry who want me to bail them out. I'm not going to do it. Nobody bailed me out. I had to learn how to use my faith, and they have to learn how to use their faith. I'll coach them, but I won't rob them of life's experiences. I know that in some cases I could write a check and be a solution. But if God doesn't tell me to write a check and I write one, I will cripple the man.

There's an expression that goes, "Give a man a fish and you feed him for a day. Teach a man to fish, and you feed him for a lifetime." It's the same principle. I tell everybody that Dr. Price didn't give me a dime until I was successful, until I proved I was good ground to sow into. You see, a lot of people have misguided expectations when they find a mentor, because they're looking for welfare. They want to know, "What are you going to give me?"

We have an organization of pastors, and I tell them up front what I'm about. I'll give them wisdom and counsel when they want it. I'm not going to go and run their church, but I'll be their coach. But when I talk to them, a lot of them don't hear that. They hear, "You have a lot of money and a big church, so you can help me get where I want to go." When they say that, I tell them, "That's not what I promised you. I'll show you where you missed it, so you can use your faith. I'm where I am in ministry because my mentor allowed me to use my faith."

That's important, because when you rise to a place of mentorship and a lot of people want something from you, you'll understand that a person's failure to plan does not make their situation your emergency.

Ways to Respect a Mentor

I must respect my mentor. How am I going to respect him? Number one, I respect him by understanding that he has a purpose and an assignment, and I must not become a distraction to him. In other words, I must never, ever distract or compete with my mentor.

I host an annual church development conference, where church leaders from around the nation and abroad, come to

FUELERS VS DRAINERS

learn church growth principles. Before I started that conference, I asked Dr. Price for his approval. I told him that God had put holding this conference on my heart, but I added that if he thought this conference would compete with his conference, FICWFM, Fellowship of Inner-City Word of Faith Ministries, I would not do it. And I meant it. He said, "Oh no, go ahead and do it. There's no conflict." And with his approval, I did it.

I was a grown man. I lived in an entirely different city and state. Couldn't I do whatever I wanted to do? No, not if I was going to respect my mentor. If I respect him, then I'm never going to compete with him.

Number two, you respect your mentor by respecting his time. Your mentor's time is valuable, so be sure to value the teaching moments. My biological father taught me that a person's time is valuable. I'll never forget that lesson. My father took my brother and me to Skid Row and drove us around. Have you ever been there? He showed us guys living on the street. He wasn't putting them down, but he said to me, "Son, I don't want you ever to be like that. I can't teach you everything you need to know. You'll come in contact with people who know more than I know. Don't waste their time." My daddy was so smart. You know, you find out later on in life that your Dad was smart. And I never wasted a mentor's time. I valued the teaching moments.

Number three, you respect a mentor by understanding that he has the right to set the terms of the relationship—you don't. Until Dr. Price said he wanted to meet with me, I didn't try to do it. In fact, I was sitting in the back of the auditorium one day during one of his meetings, and he sent somebody to tell me he wanted to have lunch with me. I wasn't running after him pestering him and asking, "Hey, Doc, where are you going to eat?"

Number four, you respect your mentor by recognizing that the mentor relationship should be mutually beneficial. How can you benefit your mentor? First, don't be a parasite. Don't be just a taker. Give to your mentor. Second, pour water over your mentor's hands. The Bible describes Elisha as a man who poured water over Elijah's hands (2 Kings 3:11). He ministered to him. Third, you benefit your mentor by respecting the Galatians 6:6 principle. Let's see what this is.

Galatians 6:6
6 Let him that is taught in the word communicate unto him that teacheth in all good things.

You're supposed to be giving your mentor some money. That's scriptural. *Communicate* doesn't mean to talk to him. In the context of this verse, the Bible is saying that you have an obligation to sow into your mentor's life.

Before I could give Doctor Price big money, I gave him small money, but I gave my small money regularly. Now, I'm regular with my big money. That's because I live by the Galatians 6:6 principle.

Fourth, I respect my mentor by always remembering that he is greater than I am. We looked at this earlier in this chapter.

Understanding the Learning Process

As the one being mentored, I must understand the learning process. This is how I learn from my mentor.

Teaching. I must hear his teaching of the Word at the level of my comprehension.

Repetition. I must hear my mentor's teaching repeatedly. Repetition is part of the learning process.

Study. I have to do some work on my own. Study is an intensive focus on information for in-depth comprehension.

Example. An example is a natural illustration that exhibits in action the principles I want to learn.

Pattern. A pattern is a proven, systematic process that produces consistent results. I wanted to learn Dr. Price's process—how he did what he did—and pattern what I did after that, because his process was proven. It worked in Los Angeles, and I could bring that same process to Houston and prove it there. Some people said it wouldn't work in Houston, but they were wrong. It was a proven process. So, I learned the process from him and I put it into effect where I lived. When the process worked in north Houston, we took it to south Houston. When the process worked there, we took it to east Houston. Then we took it to Austin and Beaumont, and it's working in those cities.

Practice. Once you understand the process, you have to practice it. You have to act out the principles and concepts that you've learned from your mentor.

Skill. When you practice the process you've learned, you'll reach a place of skill. You get so you can do it in your sleep. Mastering a process is the key to long-term effectiveness.

Loyalty

Loyalty is required both of the mentor and the one being mentored. *Loyalty* can be defined as faithfulness displayed in conduct, conversation, and contributions that remains steadfast, unwavering, and unmovable in the face of pressure to renounce or betray one's allegiance to a person or a cause. *Conduct* is what you do. *Conversation* is how you talk. *Contribution* is what you give.

Loyalty is lacking in the Body of Christ, and I don't understand it. I have a real problem with disloyalty. I don't understand how pimps and hustlers can be more loyal to each other than folks in the church are to each other. I have a problem when I see a guy willing to go to jail or even die before he will turn in his friend, and we in the Church can't be loyal to one another. We backstab. I can't understand that.

People ask me how I could have grown up in church and still know so much about the streets. I used to shine shoes at a little shoe shop on the street. All the hustlers and pimps would come by and I'd shine their shoes. I was a good shine boy, and I learned a whole lot about the streets. I saw guys shot and killed. I've been around the hustlers and the pimps, and I don't understand how we in the Church can have the Holy Ghost and the love of God inside us, and we can't stand firm with a brother. I have a real problem with that. There shouldn't be any disloyalty or backbiting. My word ought to be my bond.

Years ago when Dr. Price started talking about racism and religion, a lot of his board members jumped ship. I didn't understand that. They owed it to him to at least hear him out. I said something about what was happening on my television program. I didn't know it would be broadcast nationwide. Dr. Price heard it and put it on his television program. What I said was, "I'm standing with you. You're my mentor, and I will not betray you. I will not renounce you." Some other ministers told me that because I'd backed Dr. Price, my ministry would never get very far. I told them, "It isn't about that. It's about doing what's right."

So, how do I stay loyal to my mentor? Here are some ways.

- Never harbor an offense.
- Never reject righteous correction.
- Never manipulate others.
- Never engage in self-promotion.
- Restrain your ambition.
- Don't put down authority to promote yourself.
- Don't conspire with others who are in a place of rebellion.

The mentoring process emphasizes loyalty and faithfulness because it is the key to success. The life of my testimony is the strength of my character and integrity. Now, here's what most people don't understand about disloyalty. Disloyal people fall off the scene. Nobody talks about Judas in a positive way. Nobody talks positively about Gehazi (see 2 Kings 5:20–27), but folks are still talking about Joshua and Elijah. Loyalty and faithfulness pay off. The Bible says, "If ye have not been faithful in that which is another man's, who shall give you that which is your own?" (Luke 16:12).

In conclusion, it's important to recognize that the mentoring process is God's way of passing on from one person to another the knowledge and wisdom needed to advance His

Kingdom in the earth. Find your mentor and serve him. As you put into practice what we've looked at in this chapter about mentoring, you will be a help to your mentor, you will learn from him, and you will, in turn, be on your way to effectively mentoring others.

8

A Man and
His Ministry

In this chapter, we're going to look at a man and his ministry. We're going to consider our created purpose in the earth. Ultimate fulfillment comes when we know that God's purpose for our lives is for us to be involved in ministry. We all have a ministry. Greatness, from God's perspective, comes when a man embraces his ministry knowing that it's the divine path to promotion.

Most people don't see themselves as ministers, but the Bible tells us that God has given all of us the ministry of reconciliation (2 Cor. 5:18). So every born-again believer has a ministry.

Now let's look in the Old Testament at when God first talked to the prophet Jeremiah about his ministry.

Jeremiah 1:5–10

5 Before I formed thee in the belly I knew thee; and before thou camest forth out of the womb I sanctified thee, and I ordained thee a prophet unto the nations.

6 Then said I, Ah, Lord God! behold, I cannot speak: for I am a child.

7 But the LORD said unto me, Say not, I am a child: for thou shalt go to all that I shall send thee, and whatsoever I command thee thou shalt speak.

8 Be not afraid of their faces: for I am with thee to deliver thee, saith the LORD.

9 Then the LORD put forth his hand, and touched my mouth. And the LORD said unto me, Behold, I have put my words in thy mouth.

10 See, I have this day set thee over the nations and over the kingdoms, to root out, and to pull down, and to destroy, and to throw down, to build, and to plant.

We see here that God created Jeremiah. God told Jeremiah, "Before you were born, I knew you." In other words, God was saying to Jeremiah, "You are here on divine assignment. You have a divine purpose." Every man has to learn that he is not a mistake. He may not have been planned by his parents, but he was planned by God to be in the earth for such a time as this.

Now, you may not be living out your potential at the moment, but you have to understand that you are important to the plan of God. Other folks may not know your importance, but *you* have to know your importance. You have to come to grips with the reality that you're here for a divine reason. What God does for one in principle, He must do for another. As stated in Acts 10:34, God is no respecter of persons. God gave Jeremiah a purpose, and He will give you a purpose. You need to be in search of your purpose. We saw in an earlier chapter that your purpose is to live your life to benefit others. Your unique purpose is that you're supposed to be living out God's plan for your life. You were created and brought into the Kingdom of God so that you could get involved in good works. Your purpose in life is based in Ephesians chapter 2. Let's look there.

> Ephesians 2:10
>
> 10 For we are his workmanship, created in Christ Jesus unto good works, which God hath before ordained that we should walk in them.

So just as God had a preordained plan for Jeremiah's life, He has a preordained plan for your life. You have a universal or general purpose that can be seen in Genesis chapter 1. God created Adam to fellowship with Him and worship Him, to care for His things, and to reproduce after his own kind. So God had a general purpose for Adam, and His general purpose for me, in principle, is the same.

A Unique Purpose

Each man also has a unique purpose—a specific thing that God wants him to do—which God is obligated to reveal to him. The Word of God states in Proverbs 3:6 to in all our ways acknowledge Him and He will direct and make straight and plain our paths. God shows us here that He is committed to directing our lives in a way that pleases Him. And until God reveals that specific purpose to us, we should find a righteous vision to work under.

When God calls a group of believers together, He does it for a reason. There is a united purpose for that group. If you are in a group of believers, God has brought you together for a reason. He's orchestrated the paths of your lives to cross for a purpose. So don't take it lightly that you're where you are in life. Look in First Corinthians chapter 12.

1 Corinthians 12:18

18 But now hath God set the members every one of them in the body, as it hath pleased him.

We have been set in the Body of Christ as it has pleased God. Whatever church you are in, you've been set in that church not as it pleased you, but as it pleased God. God has been working in your life, taking you through all the things you've gone through, so that you could be where you are right now. God has deposited something in you that is needed in His Kingdom. You have to really believe that, whatever you've been through, God has guided your life and brought you to where you are.

God wanted Jeremiah to know that even though he was young and immature, He had a plan for him. And God has a plan for you too. When you see that there is a united plan for the group of believers you are in, and that God put you together for a particular reason, then when you work together, nothing will be impossible for you.

Our fulfillment in life is always inseparably linked to our God-given ministry purpose. That purpose is in the mind of the Maker, and it is His exclusive right to define it. We ought to be pursuing greatness in the Kingdom of God. And God's plan for greatness in His Kingdom is totally contrary to the greatness plan that most of us have been conditioned to follow.

Let's look at what happened when men got together and worked and focused together. We see an example of this in Genesis chapter 11.

Genesis 11:6

6 And the LORD said, Behold, the people is one, and they have all one language; and this they begin to do: and now nothing will be restrained from them, which they have imagined to do.

This statement comes from the story of the building of the tower of Babel. This was an unrighteous project. God didn't tell them to build that tower. But the principle of unity is so powerful that God had to confuse their languages so that they could not stay in one accord in this unrighteous endeavor. Had they stayed in one accord, even in this unrighteous project, they would have been able to do it. That's how powerful unity is.

Once you see this principle, you can understand why the devil sows discord everywhere he can among believers. He knows that if we can ever get in agreement and work together, there is nothing we can't do. It's a scriptural law. That's why he tries to sow confusion in your home and keep you and your wife from getting into agreement. The devil knows that if you and she get into one accord, he's in trouble.

Submitting Ourselves to God's Ministry

Will we submit ourselves to the ministry God has for us and serve Him? The Bible says if we'll be willing and obedient we'll eat the good of the land (Isa. 1:19). Job 36:11 says, "If they obey and serve him, they shall spend their days in prosperity, and their years in pleasures." The Scriptures are saying to us that to have a good life, we must serve God.

Romans 12:1 says, "I beseech you therefore, brethren, by the mercies of God, that ye present your bodies a living sacrifice, holy, acceptable unto God, which is your reasonable service." Don't come to the Kingdom of God with a "What's-in-it-for-me" attitude. Come to the Kingdom with a "What-can-I-do" attitude. We have to get rid of a consumerism mentality. We must understand that we're not in the Kingdom of God to consume its resources; we've been brought into the Kingdom because we have something to give. But we are conditioned by the world to believe otherwise. We are conditioned to believe that greatness is somebody putting us on a pedestal.

When you find out what's really important to God, you'll see that most people live totally contrary to His Word. Look in Mark chapter 9.

> Mark 9:33–35
> 33 And he came to Capernaum: and being in the house he asked them, What was it that ye disputed among yourselves by the way?
> 34 But they held their peace: for by the way they had disputed among themselves, who should be the greatest.
> 35 And he sat down, and called the twelve, and saith unto them, If any man desire to be first, the same shall be last of all, and servant of all.

Jesus said here that the one who wanted to be the greatest in God's Kingdom must be the servant of all. Jesus said something else about greatness in Matthew chapter 5.

Matthew 5:19

19 Whosoever therefore shall break one of these least commandments, and shall teach men so, he shall be called the least in the kingdom of heaven: but whosoever shall do and teach them, the same shall be called great in the kingdom of heaven.

On another occasion, the mother of two of Jesus' disciples went to Him with her sons to see if she could get seats for them on His left hand and right hand (Matt. 20:20–28). Jesus told them, "No, I can't do that. That is not Mine to give." The other disciples heard about it and jumped on those two guys. They said, "What are you doing, going behind our backs and trying to get ahead of us and get Jesus to say that when He sets up His Kingdom, you'll be on His left and right?" Jesus heard them disputing and said, "Hey, fellows, you've got it all wrong. God's Kingdom doesn't operate like that. You think that greatness is having people serve you. But greatness in God's Kingdom is you serving others."

The Formula for Greatness

The formula for greatness in the Kingdom of God is "Do, Teach, and Serve." You do the Word. You teach others to do it. And you serve. You serve God by serving others. Jesus said, "What you've done to the least of these, you've done unto Me." (Matt. 25:40.) So your mentality has to change. You have to have a paradigm shift in your thinking if you're going to be great in the Kingdom of God. You must understand that ministry to others is the greatest thing you can do, because Jesus died for people, and people are important to Him.

Jesus illustrated greatness because He came to serve. Our whole way of thinking has to change so that we don't have a consumer mentality but a servant mentality. God blesses those who will serve others.

We see examples of this truth in the lives of Solomon and Job. Solomon's great wealth was a divine response to his having a heart to bless others. God asked him, "What do you want?" (1 Kings 3:5–14). Solomon said, "I just need wisdom and knowledge so I can serve Your people." And God said, "Since you didn't ask for money, I'll give you wisdom and knowledge. But on top of that, I'll give you more riches than any man has ever had." And the Bible says that Job's whole situation turned around when he got his eyes off his problems and started interceding for his friends (Job 42:10).

I cannot lose by being a servant to others. Look at the following verse from Ephesians chapter 6.

Ephesians 6:8
8 Knowing that whatsoever good thing any man doeth, the same shall he receive of the Lord, whether he be bond or free.

Every man ought to know this verse. This tells me that I have a divine contract. Whatever I make happen for others, God will make happen for me.

God's Plan for Greatness

God requires three elements for His greatness plan for us to be fulfilled. *First, He requires our bodies.* We see this in two scripture passages. First, look in Romans chapter 12.

Romans 12:1

1 I beseech you therefore, brethren, by the mercies of God, that ye present your bodies a living sacrifice, holy, acceptable unto God, which is your reasonable service.

The Bible tells us here that God wants us to present our bodies as a living sacrifice. In other words, He has a right to my body. Look at these next two verses in First Corinthians.

1 Corinthians 6:19–20

19 What? know ye not that your body is the temple of the Holy Ghost which is in you, which ye have of God, and ye are not your own?

20 For ye are bought with a price: therefore glorify God in your body, and in your spirit, which are God's.

This scripture says that we have been bought with a price. We are not our own. We're to give ourselves up to Him and say, "Okay, God, I'm Yours. What do you want me to do? I'm willing to do whatever you want."

Some folks see me at the level I'm at now and tell me, "Well, that's easy for *you* to say." But they don't understand that I didn't start out at this level. Nobody flagged me down and said, "There's this big church over here with all these buildings, and all these people want you to be their pastor." I used to clean the toilets. I used to be the janitor. My wife and I hung the sheet rock. That's one reason I'm so good to her. She stuck with me. She helped me hang, tape, and float that sheet rock. We did it all. Because there's nothing I won't do for the success of the Kingdom.

To activate His greatness plan for our lives, God first requires our physical bodies. *Second, He requires our best.* We can't give Him just anything.

- Our best is based on our character. What does best mean for me? I should give God no less than what I require.

- Our best is based on comparison to a standard. When one thing is better than another, God always deserves the better.

- Our best has to do with our conscience. Only I know when I've given my best.

- Our best has to do with the criteria. I measure up to or exceed whatever criteria have been set.

God requires my body. He requires my best. *And third, He requires my boldness.* Men in the Body of Christ ought not to be sissies, punks, and wimps. We ought to be bold men of God. Boldness has to do with a conviction that leads to action against the odds. We read in the Bible about all the victories that men and women of God won. But to achieve them, they had to be bold, and we have to be bold. In other words, we have to follow God's Word even when it looks like the odds are against us.

How to Make a Godly Man

How do you produce a man who lets God be Lord over his body, who gives God his best, and who follows God's Word against all odds? How do you produce this type of man? First, you do it through the law of environment. A man's environment is critical to him excelling and exceeding in ministry.

A man's environment is the specific sphere of exposure and influence on his life. What I'm exposed to—the people and things I'm around and the places I go to—impacts my perspective on life, or how I see life. Those influences impact my performance, or what I do in life. What I'm exposed to impacts my productivity, or what I achieve in life. My environment is critical to God's greatness plan for me. I have to understand how to properly judge my environment, because *my environment will change me before I change it.* That's the first factor about the law of environment that we have to consider. A law always works the same way, so I have to make sure that I'm in the right environment, or I could be working against myself. Look at this verse in First Corinthians chapter 15.

> 1 Corinthians 15:33
> 33 Be not deceived: evil communications corrupt good manners.

The Amplified Bible says it this way.

> 1 Corinthians 15:33
> 33 Do not be so deceived and misled! Evil companionships (communion, associations) corrupt and deprave good manners and morals and character.

Your companionships are your buddies—the folks you hang out with. The Bible tells me that an evil environment will change me before I change it. That's why brothers who have just come out of drug addiction shouldn't go back and try to save the folks at the crack house. They aren't ready yet. Those brothers are all fired up, but they aren't ready to go back around that environment

The second factor we need to consider about the law of environment is, *our environment will cause us to either blossom or be barren.* Your environment will either cause you to fulfill your potential, or it will shut you down.

The third factor about the law of environment that we need to look at is, *our environment is a silent, prophetic declaration that speaks to our future.* Whoever I allow to influence my life is giving direction to my destiny. When I look at them, I can tell where I'm going. In other words, I'm like an arrow and they're pointing me somewhere, and where I'm going is where they've already gone. I need to look at who I'm allowing to influence my life, and I have to decide, *Do I want to be like that?* And if I don't want to be like that, I have to change my environment.

When we were growing up, our parents tried to keep us around certain folks. We thought they were trying to be mean and didn't want us to have any fun. We didn't know any better. Had we known better, we would have listened. Most of us can think of a time when we wouldn't have gotten into some kind of trouble that we did get into if we hadn't been with the people we were with. Look at this verse in First Corinthians.

1 Corinthians 5:6

6 Your glorying is not good. Know ye not that a little leaven leaveneth the whole lump?

The Apostle Paul was talking about environment. I have to judge my environment; I cannot change it. If I stay with my environment long enough, it will change me.

The Holy Spirit wants to flood your life with the right environment—the right influences. One of the most powerful lessons I learned years ago was that I had to be in the right environment. All of us are like seeds. We are preprogrammed to produce what God has put in us, but that program is not released until we're in the right environment. A seed is programmed to produce a certain thing, but the program is not activated until that seed is in the right environment—the soil. Once that seed is in the right environment, that environment triggers something in the seed and gives something to it so the seed germinates and begins to grow. It's the same with you. When you're in the right environment, something happens to you.

So I have to look at my environment. When my heart is right toward God and my desire is to please Him, God is obligated to bring me into the company of the people I need to know and give me the knowledge that I need that is critical to my success and destiny in life. I believe that the Holy Spirit leads me into the right environment.

How do I judge my environment? *First, I need to be around people who live according to purpose.* Since I want to follow my purpose, I need to be around others who live according to purpose. *Second, I need to be around those whose lives are productive.* I need to be around folks who are doing something, and who have something to show for what they're doing. *Third, I need to be around those who think progressively.* I don't need to be around a lot of pessimistic thinkers. I don't need to be around people who are always saying, "It's so hard. It's so tough. Nobody will give me a break."

Fourth, I need to be around those who live by principle. Since I want to live by principle, and I understand that proven principles will cause the same results in my life that they have in others' lives, I need to be around people who are governed by principle, not by passion. So *fifth, I need to be around people who can control their passion.* I need to be around folks who can resist temptation and not always fall. *Sixth, I need to be around people who have the strength of character to promote others*—people who won't be jealous if I have a new suit and they don't. I don't need to be around folks who can't rejoice with me. I need to be around people who are able to promote others, even if God takes me higher than they are.

So I test my environment against God's standard. I test the folks I hang with. What I do with the results depends on where I really want to go in life, because when I test my environment, I may find that I'm hanging with the wrong group. That doesn't mean I think I'm better than they are, but I have somewhere I'm going, so I have to redefine some relationships. I can't hang with them. Oh, we can be casual friends, but we can't spend quality time together, because I'm on a mission now.

Handling My Relationships

After I analyze my relationships, there are some decisions I have to make about them. *First, there are some relationships I must regulate.* I have to install some guidelines for the sake of my commitment. If I'm committed to God and someone else isn't, and that other person doesn't want to go where I want to go, then I've got to regulate that relationship. *Second, there are some relationships I must initiate.* I need to find the right group to hang with. I need to find a group of strong, godly men. *Third, there are some relationships I must totally eliminate.* I have to terminate them because those people are a corrupting influence.

Maybe you wouldn't have a police record if you hadn't hung around with certain people. Maybe you wouldn't have gotten into drugs if that other person hadn't been giving them to you. Maybe you and your wife would still be together if that other guy hadn't messed with her.

Fourth, there are some relations I must cultivate. I have to improve these relationships for maximum return.

When we really understand the law of environment, we'll do whatever we need to do to get connected and stay connected with the right people and influences. Our God-ordained, God-created purpose is at stake. That's why we all need to be in a good church. We must value the local church because if it's a good church, that environment will edify us. A good church is not going to make us feel good all the time. A good church ought to *challenge* us through its faithful example and calling. It ought to *change* us through the anointed ministry of the Word. It ought to *correct* us when we need a loving rebuke and exhortation. And it ought to *care for* us through the personal ministry of the saints.

Now look at this verse in Luke chapter 16.

Luke 16:12
12 And if ye have not been faithful in that which is another man's, who shall give you that which is your own?

Here are seven principles for maximizing your ministry. Remember: you're called to ministry. Your first spiritual ministry to the world ought to be in your local church. Of course, you know your first ministry is at home, but we're not looking at that ministry right now. We're looking at living out this calling of the ministry of reconciliation that God has given us, and it's lived out in your church.

- *Expose yourself to successful others who will share their testimonies.* I need to be around folks who will tell me about what God has done in their lives.

- *Eliminate negative influences that discourage you from dreaming.* I don't need to be around anybody who is going to put down my dream. Years ago I made the choice. I had to cut a whole lot of people loose from my life when I left the denomination I was in. Now please— doing that is not for everybody. I knew what God had told me to do, and a lot of people were telling me it wasn't going to work. Well, I couldn't stay around them. They were talking against my dream.

- *Expand your knowledge to eradicate misconceptions and myths.* In other words, there are places that my body may not be able to go to, but I can take my mind there when I read. I need to expand my thinking.

- *Exemplify and model the success plan of others based on principles.* I don't need to reinvent the wheel. If somebody else tells me what worked for them, I'll work it for myself.

- *Exhort others to pursue their goals and dreams so someone will exhort you.* What I make happen for others, God will make happen for me. So if I want encouragement, I give encouragement. I'm not going to just sit around looking for someone to encourage me. I'm going to encourage somebody else.

- *Emancipate yourself from past failures and mistakes that seem to disqualify you from success.* You may have failed in the past, but that doesn't mean you're going to fail in the future.

- *Embrace the ministry of your mentor as a seed for God to promote you.*

When you as a man of God surrender to the high calling of being a minister in the Kingdom of God, you'll see transformation in your home, your church, and your community. You'll experience a whole new level of fulfillment and wholeness as you begin to live to benefit others. Blessings will rebound bountifully into your life!

9

A Man and His Money

My purpose in this chapter is to enlighten men on the principles of financial management in the Kingdom of God. It's about stewardship. I want to ignite faith in you for financial abundance and wealth as promised in the Word of God. The Scriptures tell us to trust God to provide for us, and to expect Him to do that liberally. We see that in this verse in First Timothy.

1 Timothy 6:17

17 Charge them that are rich in this world, that they be not highminded, nor trust in uncertain riches, but in the living God, who giveth us richly all things to enjoy.

We're looking at a man and his money. The importance of money in any society can never be underestimated, especially in the society we live in. We have to have some money if we're going to take care of our families and our business.

Maximizing our financial state is a matter of information and discipline. As we read through the Bible, it's very easy to see that it is God's will for us to have some finances. What we call the Book of First Timothy is a letter the Apostle Paul wrote to Timothy, the pastor of a church. In chapter 6 and verse 17, Paul says to Timothy, "Instruct those who are rich in this world." So there were some rich folks in the New Testament Church. There's nothing wrong with being rich. In the church I pastor, I don't have to spend much time on this point. But as I travel around the country, I'm amazed at how many people don't know whether they're supposed to have anything. The Word of God says that we are. It's God's will for us to have more than enough.

But Paul told Timothy to tell the rich people in his church not to trust in riches. God showed me how not to trust in riches. If you trust in money, you'll always be nervous about it, because our society has taught men to equate their worth with what they have in their pocket and in their bank account.

We've been trained to associate our value with our money, so whenever a man spends money, some of his worth goes with it. That's why it can be hard for a man to spend his money. Yes, he wants the best for his wife and children, but he doesn't want to part with his money sometimes because he has associated his worth with it.

Sometimes when a man has to spend his money, he gets angry and he doesn't know why. He's not aware that his worth is tied up in that money. A paradigm shift needs to take place in his thinking. His worth and value needs to be tied to his relationship with God, not to his money.

Money in the earth is like a river. There's no shortage of money. You may not have enough right now. You may not have an abundance in your pocket, but there's no shortage of it.

There's plenty of money in the earth. You have to get rid of stinginess. You may not have much money now, but your thinking is controlling your ability to acquire it. If you're thinking in terms of lack and limitation, it's difficult for you to think in terms of surplus. You can't think surplus and lack at the same time. God's plan to bring us to a place of abundance is in His Word, and since we've made Him Lord, we need to follow His plan. The point I want you to see now is, there's plenty of money in the earth.

People become jealous of the success of others when they have a pie mentality concerning money. In other words, their view is that there's only so much money, and whoever gets a piece of the pie will be okay. If you grew up with brothers and sisters or you had cousins, you might understand this. When there were a lot of people at the house and dessert time came and the adults got ready to cut the cake or the pie, you counted everybody. You did a quick assessment in your head and you figured out that because there were so many people, you were going to get less. A poverty mentality says there's only so much available, and when you get some that means there's less for me. If you have a poverty mentality about money, you cannot rejoice when others have it.

Money Is Like a River

God told me that money is like a river flowing in the earth, and all of us are like landowners who own parcels of land next to the river. He who knows how best to draw that water off to irrigate his land gets the benefit of the water. If you don't use it to irrigate, it'll pass you by, but there's no shortage.

God has given each of us a talent, a skill, a way to tap into the river of finances that's flowing by us. To the degree that we maximize what God has given us, we'll receive the abundance He has promised.

When pleasing God is the object of my affection, I step into the flow of God's power, provision, and protection to bring His purposes to pass in my generation. When I'm pleasing God, He's filling my life with stuff. Look at this verse in the Book of Proverbs.

Proverbs 10:22

22 The blessing of the LORD, it maketh rich, and he addeth no sorrow with it.

When someone says to me, "It isn't the will of God for everybody to be rich," my question to them is, "Who is this verse not for?" It bothers me when I see preachers interviewed on TV and they say that it's not God's will for everybody to have abundance. Somebody who doesn't understand what the Bible says about prosperity does not have the right to deny prosperity to somebody else.

Deuteronomy 8:18 says, "But thou shalt remember the LORD thy God: for it is he that giveth thee power to get wealth...." Because the Bible says that, I can boldly state that God has given you sufficient skills and talents to prosper. Those skills and talents may not have manifested yet, but you have what it takes to tap into the river of finances so you can have more than enough. All *rich* means is that you'll have enough for yourself and enough to help somebody else, with some left over. That's what abundance is. To be rich is to be abundantly supplied. So my thinking has to change. Until that happens, nothing else is going to change.

Kingdom Mandates

There are three Kingdom mandates that come into play as we consider a man and his money: principles of the Kingdom, provision for the Kingdom, and provision for the family. The Bible says that a man ought to work so he can have something to give to someone in need (Eph. 4:28). If you're a man of God—a Kingdom man—and you've made Jesus Lord, then He's Lord over all or He's not Lord at all. If you've made Him your Lord, that means He's Lord over your money too. You need to see yourself as being in the Kingdom of God to promote the Kingdom, and as making money so you can advance the Kingdom.

We already know that it's God's will that we tithe. The tithe came before the Law (Gen. 14:18–20, 28:22), was incorporated into the Law, and continued after the Law (Heb. 7:8). In Matthew 23:23, Jesus told the scribes and Pharisees that they should have been tithing. And one purpose of the tithe is that there be provision for God's house. Look at this verse in Malachi chapter 3.

> Malachi 3:10
> 10 Bring ye all the tithes into the storehouse, that there may be meat in mine house….

We are to properly manage our resources so that there can be meat, or provision, in God's house. In Luke chapter 8, we see that there were people who ministered to Jesus out of their substance (vv. 2–3). Second Corinthians 9:10–11 says that the end result of my increase should be my participation in an abundance of good works. The first thing a Kingdom man has to understand is that God blesses him so he can be a blessing. I cannot partake of Abraham's blessings without partaking of his agenda. And that agenda was, he was blessed to be a blessing.

Another reason God causes me to prosper is so that I can provide for my family. Look at this verse in First Timothy chapter 5.

> 1 Timothy 5:8
> 8 But if any provide not for his own, and specially for those of his own house, he hath denied the faith, and is worse than an infidel.

I said earlier that, all things being equal, I don't understand men who don't want to work. I'm not talking about men who are disabled or sick. I'm saying that if I'm healthy, then it's God's will for me to work. Work is expending my energies and my intellectual and physical efforts for a productive return or, in other words, for increase. If I get paid for playing basketball, that's work. If I play basketball and nobody is paying me, then basketball is not work for me. I can define work as something that I do that I get paid for. I'm being compensated for it. Money's coming in. If money isn't coming in, I'm not working.

If you have a straight commission job and you aren't getting any commission, then you aren't working. You may be showing up, but some money has to be coming in for it to be work. God said in First Timothy 5:8 that if you don't provide for your own, you have denied the faith and you are worse than an infidel.

Husbands Should Take Care of Their Wives

I'm going to tell it like it is. If you're married, your wife shouldn't be taking care of you. You should be taking care of your wife. One day when I was pastoring a small church and not much money was coming in, my wife came to me and said she would take care of me. She had a little job, but most of her income was going to babysitters and so on. I told her, "Call them tomorrow at that job. You will not go back." I was responsible to take care of her, and I did. Yes, I was walking by faith, but I made sure there was money coming in.

Don't tell me you're walking by faith if you're not bringing any money in. You need a job until your faith can produce in other ways. I'm not telling you to give up your dream. I'm telling you that if you're not providing now for your family, you need to do that.

Now if a man and his wife have agreed that they're both going to work and bring in money, then she would be wrong to quit her job and leave her husband with the bills. They made those bills together. For her to quit, they'd have to plan it. They might have to scale back their lifestyle because they incurred those bills based on two incomes, but a man is supposed to provide for his family.

I was willing to do whatever I had to do to provide for my family. I did manual labor. I was a "roughneck" in the oil fields. That's a tough job. I remember the first day I showed up for work. I had a suit on. The foreman came out, a plug of chewing tobacco in his jaw, and said, "You don't need a suit." He handed me a 48-inch pipe wrench and said, "All you need here is a strong back and a willing mind." For my first task, he drew a square on the ground and told me to dig a ditch. I spent all day digging that ditch. I got it perfect. At the end of the day, he blew the whistle and somebody drove a bulldozer over and filled it in. That was my initiation. In other words, they were telling me, "You can't care about what happens. You just do what we tell you to do." Married men are supposed to provide for their families. Now look at this verse in Proverbs chapter 13.

> Proverbs 13:22
> 22 A good man leaveth an inheritance to his children's children: and the wealth of the sinner is laid up for the just.

The Bible defines a good man as one who will leave an inheritance not only for his children but for his children's children. When you die, will it be a sad day for everybody? I told my family, "At my funeral, I want you all to cry. I want some tears. And on the way to the grave, you can all cry a little bit. But when you're on your way back from the grave and you think about what I left you, you ought to be singing 'Oh Happy Day'."

Every man ought to have life insurance. Don't make your family wish they could bury your body in the backyard to save money. Real men have insurance. I'm serious. We've had members of our church who had no insurance die, and the children had to come up with enough money to bury them.

A Kingdom Mentality

I want us to look now at a Kingdom mentality as it relates to a man and his money. Romans 12:2 tells us to renew our minds. We see the same thought in Third John 2: "Beloved, I wish above all things that thou mayest prosper and be in health, even as thy soul prospereth." The mind is part of the soul, and my mind prospers as I renew it with God's Word. I have to renew my mind to think in line with the Word of God. I need to remove limited thinking about material prosperity and blessing because I cannot rise above how I think. My faith won't operate beyond that.

I've been in a situation where having a little is less intimidating than having a lot, but I must understand that God wants me to have more. I was taught that bigness is bad and abundance is waste. A lot of other folks have been taught that way too. What's wrong with big? Would you want me to give you a one-dollar bill or a hundred-dollar bill? Nothing's wrong with big, but people are intimidated by it. I have to start thinking big. We assume that extravagance is ungodly. I don't know where we got that from. People who think that haven't read the Bible. Look in the Bible at how God dressed up Heaven (see Rev. 21:9–27). Streets of gold. Walls of jasper. Gates made of pearl. God isn't cutting back. He loves extravagance.

We also have been taught to think pessimistically about money. Haven't you heard in church that money is the root of all evil? This scripture has been misquoted for years. The Bible clearly says in 1 Timothy 6:10 that the *love of money* is the root of all evil.

Eradicating Money-Mismanagement Thinking

I have to change my thinking. Unless I eradicate money-mismanagement thinking, I'm going to continue to mismanage my money. There are a number of wrong ways to think about money that cause me to mismanage it.

Greed. Greed is being dissatisfied with what I have and lusting for more.

Grief. Grief over money is when I see giving as a loss and not as an investment. That's the kind of thinking that the rich synagogue ruler who came to Jesus had (see Luke 18:18–23.)

Gimmicks. A gimmick is something unrighteous that I do to get money.

Gangster. A gangster is a person who will not give but attempts to get money by unrighteous means. Judas had a gangster's heart. He wanted to get gain by unrighteous means. He was a thief.

Get Over. Somebody with a "get-over" attitude, an attitude that causes people to believe they can get something for nothing, gives that which is of little or no value. Cain tried to get over. He gave God something which was of no value to him, and God said, "I don't want that."

Guarantee. Someone with a guarantee mentality thinks that benefits are guaranteed to him because he's related to somebody who's getting the benefits. This is the kind of thinking that the prophet Eli's boys had (see 1 Sam. 2:12–36). Eli's sons thought they could get the Lord's benefits through their relationship with their father, without going through the process of obeying the Lord. When my adult children give in church, I'm not standing in the back giving them money. I taught them that if they're going to be blessed, it's not going to happen by them hanging on to my coattails. *They* have to give, and God will bless them because they give.

I taught my kids the principle that Daddy got to where he is by giving. If you want to get to where Daddy is, you'll have to do the same thing. You'll have to go through the process and not expect that you have a guarantee that you will prosper just because of who I am. The Kingdom of God doesn't work like that.

Grudgeful. A grudgeful giver gives with an irate attitude. It's as if he's saying, "I don't want to give this, but here it is anyway." The Bible says God doesn't want grudgeful gifts; He wants cheerful gifts (see 2 Cor. 9:6–7).

If we think about money in any of these ungodly ways, we will mismanage the money we have.

Kingdom Ways to Deal With Money

The Bible tells me how to deal with my money. Let's look first at how the Scriptures tell me I'm to receive money. Here are five biblical ways:

1. Work
2. Investments
3. Inheritance
4. Gifts
5. Compensation

By compensation I mean compensation for damages. That's in the order and plan of God. In the Old Testament, when a person was damaged physically, financially, or in some other way, he was to receive compensation for that damage.

The Bible tells me six things I'm supposed to do with my money, in the following order.

1. Support the Kingdom of God (Prov. 3:10).
2. Pay taxes (Rom. 13:7; Mark 12:17).
3. Repay my debts (2 Kings 4:7; Matt. 17:24–27).
4. Pay my living expenses (1 Tim. 5:8).
5. Accumulate and save (Prov. 6:6).
6. Give to the poor (Prov. 19:17; Eph. 4:28).

I give to God first. Then I pay my taxes. The way our society is, the government doesn't let you make that decision. They withhold their share from your paycheck before you get it. If you're self-employed, God can come first, but remember that He expects you to pay your taxes.

The third item on the list is paying your debts. If I understand that my debts become an obligation for me, I'll be careful how deep I get into debt. A man of God can't just say to his creditors, "You can't get blood out of a turnip." No, a man of God pays his debts. I have to pay my bills because my credit is the report card of my character.

Then come my living expenses. After that I accumulate and save, and then I give to the poor.

Kingdom Millionaire Status

The pathway to Kingdom millionaire status starts with seed-faith giving. I teach a series I call "Who Wants to Be a Kingdom Millionaire?" You can be a Kingdom millionaire. I've committed myself to raising up millionaires.

You can't raise anybody to a level that you haven't reached yourself. I gave away a million dollars last year. When people criticize me for teaching prosperity, I tell them, "You match my giving into the Kingdom and then I'll talk to you. But until you match my giving, I don't want to hear what you have to say."

I'm blessed, but I'm blessed to be a blessing. I have a right to teach prosperity. You see, years ago when I heard Luke 6:38, I didn't hear it like most people do. Luke 6:38 says, "Give, and it shall be given unto you; good measure, pressed down, and shaken together, and running over, shall men give into your bosom. For with the same measure that ye mete withal it shall be measured to you again."

Most people hear that verse and say, "God, raise up somebody to help me." I said, "God, raise me up and I'll help others." In order for money to get to you, it has to come through the hands of a man. The Bible says, "...shall *men* give into your bosom." Money isn't going to fall on you out of the sky. It's going to come through men giving into your bosom. My prayer to God was, "Make me the man." I took a whole other approach to that verse. I told God, "You raise me up and when you tell me to write the check, I'll write the check."

We're talking about a Kingdom millionaire. You see, a Kingdom millionaire understands that God has made him rich to be a blessing in the Kingdom. Oh, he's going to have something left over. He's not going to be broke. Some of the men in the church I pastor have already seen this happen in their lives. Some of them are giving away more now than what their entire salary was when they first came to the church. And they're not lacking. They demonstrated to God that they could be trusted with more.

Maybe you're reading this and thinking that I'm in another world because I'm talking about being rich. It's the will of God for you to be rich. I'm not talking about "pep-rally rich" where somebody pumps you up. I'm talking about seriously rich. I'm talking about your understanding how to maximize your potential so you do not have to live from week to week. It is a product of information and discipline. The discipline is, I don't live above what my faith can manifestly produce. It may not be time yet for the Mercedes. That's all right. I'll drive my Buick, and rejoice with another brother who got his Mercedes.

Keep in mind, though, you don't know how that other guy got that Mercedes. He may be driving that car but have all his windows open at his house because he can't afford air-conditioning. He may have compromised the quality of his life so he can be seen in that car. Don't let that bother you.

For years I'd go to conferences and see other guys get up and give big money. That didn't bother me. I gave what I had. I knew where I was going. Now I can give big money. But you have to understand that you can have abundance. You have to saturate your thinking with what God's Word has to say about this, because the news is usually about how things are getting worse. If you absorb that, it will kill your faith. You *can* have abundance!

If you're not there in your thinking, I'm not putting you down. When I give my testimony, I'm not trying to build me up as something great, but I know what it's like. I came up out of poverty and out of thinking I couldn't have anything. Thank

God, somebody told me I could. I fought the fight of faith. Even when it looked like nothing was changing, I kept at it. I wasn't going to be denied. I wasn't going to sit on what God gave me. He gave me what He gives everybody else: a seed. You see, that seed is more than a dollar in my pocket. It's invested potential. I'm programmed for riches. So are you. You just haven't tapped into it yet. Look at these verses in Second Corinthians chapter 9.

> Second Corinthians 9:6–8
>
> 6 But this I say, He which soweth sparingly shall reap also sparingly; and he which soweth bountifully shall reap also bountifully.
>
> 7 Every man according as he purposeth in his heart, so let him give; not grudgingly, or of necessity: for God loveth a cheerful giver.
>
> 8 And God is able to make all grace abound toward you; that ye, always having all sufficiency in all things, may abound to every good work.

Verse 7 says God loves a cheerful giver. To be a Kingdom millionaire, you have to be a giver. That's all there is to it. Verse 8 says that God makes sure I have plenty so I can give to every good work.

The point is, I have been created by God and brought into His Kingdom not just for my abundance but for the abundance of the Kingdom. When I set my heart to increase the Kingdom of God, then God will cause me to increase big time. That's His system. It doesn't matter if the world doesn't like it and people try to mock me. It's God's system.

How to Change

In order to change, I first have to be honest with myself. I need to *consider* where I'm at. Have I given life my all? Or have I done just enough to get by? I need to understand that even if I give my all in one field, if I don't reap in that field, I will reap in another field.

Second, I must have a *conviction*—an internal witness—that even though I may be outside of God's plan for handling money now, I am not going to stay outside His plan. I'm going to get into His plan. If I can trust Him for Heaven, I can trust Him to handle my resources.

Third, I'm going to change my *confession.* I'm going to bring my heart and mouth into agreement with God's Word even though it may not look like what it says will happen is happening. Years ago I began to confess that I was rich. I confessed, "The blessing of the Lord makes me rich, and He adds no sorrow with it" (Prov. 10:22). When I would say it, my mind would laugh at me. My mind would say, "Boy, you are really crazy." But I kept on, and God's Word became a reality in my life.

Fourth, I'm going to have *corresponding action*—I'm going to act on the principles that I'm learning.

Fifth, I'm going to have *consistency and courage.* I'm going to keep confessing God's Word and acting on its principles until I get results.

The Bible says of a righteous man, "Wealth and riches shall be in his house…" (Ps. 112:3). Believe that. Keep confessing that. Keep acting consistently and courageously on God's principles for abundance. And don't quit until you see abundance manifested in your life.

10

A Man and His Mind

In this chapter we'll deal with a man and his mind. My objective is to get you to appreciate the mind that God has given you and to think on another level, because what keeps you from where God wants you to go is your thinking. The Scriptures say, "As a man thinketh in his heart, so is he" (Prov. 23:7). The Bible tells me not to be conformed to the world, but to be transformed into a kingdom man by the renewing of my mind. We've already looked at a couple of these verses in Romans chapter 12, but let's go back to them.

Romans 12:1–3

1 I beseech you therefore, brethren, by the mercies of God, that ye present your bodies a living sacrifice, holy, acceptable unto God, which is your reasonable service.

2 And be not conformed to this world: but be ye transformed by the renewing of your mind, that ye may prove what is that good, and acceptable, and perfect, will of God.

3 For I say, through the grace given unto me, to every man that is among you, not to think of himself more highly than

he ought to think; but to think soberly, according as God hath dealt to every man the measure of faith.

The renewing of your mind did not happen at the new birth. When you were born again, your spirit became alive to God, but your thinking did not change. However you thought when you were a sinner is the way you thought after you were born again, until your mind was renewed.

So much in the Bible addresses the mind, and that's what we're looking at here. Maybe you've heard the saying, "A mind is a terrible thing to waste." I think that statement applies to the Body of Christ. Most believers are so spirit-minded—so spiritual—that they don't think. There is nothing more potent in the earth than a born-again man whose mind is yielded to the Spirit of God.

My mind is involved in my decision-making. It's involved in my decisions for advancement. It's involved when I'm dealing with adversity. It's involved in my decisions for abundance. So, I have to appreciate my mind.

The light came on for me years ago on this. When I became a full-time pastor, somehow I thought that I wasn't supposed to think anymore. I thought I was supposed to abandon the practical knowledge that I had learned from working in industry and just be spiritual. So I got really spiritual. Then one day I saw one of my mentors whom I was watching and learning from do some practical things. I knew how to do the things he was doing, but I wasn't doing them because I didn't know that I was supposed to be practical in my application of spiritual principles, so that's what I want to cover here.

According to First Thessalonians 5:23, man is a three-part being. He is a spirit being; he lives inside a physical body; and he possesses a soul. The soul of man that the Bible talks about has five components: his mind, his will, his imagination, his emotions, and his intellect. These five components make up a man's soul, and he will only prosper in life relative to how he develops in these five areas. We see prosperity and health linked to the development of the soul in the Book of Third John.

3 John 2
2 Beloved, I wish above all things that thou mayest prosper and be in health, even as thy soul prospereth.

The Bible has a lot to say about developing my soul. I will only experience the manifested blessing of God to the degree that I develop my soul: my mind, my will, my imagination, my emotions, and my intellect. The Bible uses many terms that relate to thinking. When the Scriptures refer to *soul, mind, looking, seeking,* or *believing,* for instance, all these faculties involve the mind.

According to the Bible, how I focus and control my mind determines my emotional state. We see this mentioned in Isaiah chapter 26.

Isaiah 26:3
3 Thou wilt keep him in perfect peace, whose mind is stayed on thee: because he trusteth in thee.

Here I see that the amount of peace I experience is determined by the focus of my mind. Most people don't use their minds. They've been reduced to robots. They're just going through the motions, and they're not being all that God created them to be.

We have to stimulate our minds. It's amazing what we can produce once we understand the mechanics of our minds. Let's look at another passage of scripture that deals with the mind. We find it in Second Corinthians chapter 10.

> 2 Corinthians 10:3–4
>
> 3 For though we walk in the flesh, we do not war after the flesh:
>
> 4 (For the weapons of our warfare are not carnal, but mighty through God to the pulling down of strong holds.)

The strongholds mentioned in verse 4 are thought patterns that keep you from God's best. They're ways of thinking that you've been conditioned to accept that keep you from achieving, and from accepting God's plan for your life. Before you came to the Lord, your head got messed up. Folks messed up your mind with their erroneous beliefs and myths and old-school thinking, and they didn't know they were doing it. Your mind became infused and contaminated with a way of thinking that is contrary to God. That's what a stronghold is. Maybe you think, *A woman can't tell me anything!* That's a stronghold. You're listening to *you* got you into the fix you're in. You *should* have listened to her. Maybe you think, *Nobody'll give a brother a break.* That's a stronghold. Maybe you've heard, "Every black man's lazy. And no white man likes a black man." Those are strongholds. They're lies. These are all things that get down into your thinking that have to be uprooted. Now look at the next verse in Second Corinthians chapter 10.

2 Corinthians 10:5

5 Casting down imaginations, and every high thing that exalteth itself against the knowledge of God, and bringing into captivity every thought to the obedience of Christ.

Notice that we're to bring *every* thought into line with God's way of thinking. That means I have to work on my mind. Proverbs 23:7 says, "As a man thinketh in his heart, so is he." When I understand that, I see that I have my work cut out for me as a believer, because I have to control my mind.

Man's Thinking Has Been Restricted

We see in the Scriptures how God created man and how man's thinking has been compromised and restricted. The Bible shows us the following three things about man's God-given creative genius:

- It is chronicled in the covenant.
- It is crippled by carnality.
- It is compromised by clutter.

First we see the creative genius of man chronicled in the covenant. The Word of God is our covenant—the Old Covenant and the New Covenant. You can see in the Scriptures how smart God made man. God gave Adam the genius to name every beast of the field and every fowl of the air. The Bible says that God brought all these animals to Adam to see what he would call them. Whatever Adam called each animal, that was its name (Gen. 2:19). A little later you see Nimrod. The Bible calls him a mighty hunter (Gen. 10:9). If you study the Old Covenant, you see that Nimrod was a man of color and was leading the whole known world at that time. He was leading them the wrong way, but he was leading them. In fact, he had a plan to build a tower, and his plan was so masterful that God had to come down and interfere with him so he wouldn't complete what he was doing.

Second, the creative genius of man is crippled by his carnality. Thinking which is solely based on natural knowledge and instincts, which are earthly and fleshly, is void of the wisdom of God. Now remember that Second Corinthians 10:5 tells us to bring every thought into the obedience of Christ. My thinking must come in line with how God wants me to think. So when we talk about creative thinking, we don't mean going off on some tangent. The Word of God is the standard for how I'm supposed to think. I need to bring all my thoughts into line with this Word.

Third, man's creative thinking is compromised by clutter. Some men have so many unnecessary and foolish things in their heads that they can't think right. They have their minds cluttered with pornography and they see mental images of naked women. Or they have their minds cluttered with worries, and they can't think creatively as God wants them to. A cluttered mind can cause you to waver. We see the effects of a wavering mind in the Book of James.

James 1:7–8
7 For let not that man think that he shall receive any thing of the Lord.
8 A double minded man is unstable in all his ways.

I have to learn how to think so I can eliminate the clutter in my mind. Clutter can keep me from sleeping. It can keep me from making accurate decisions. When my mind is cluttered, I can't consider everything I need to consider, and I make a bad decision and end up with an "oops" on my table. Remember what an oops is? An oops happens when I made a bad decision and experience some bad consequences, and I say, "Oops, I wish I hadn't done that." To eliminate the oopses in my life, I have to be able to think correctly. To do that, I must eliminate the clutter in my mind.

The Bible gives us snapshots of men who learned to maximize their minds. Three of them are David, Nehemiah, and the Apostle Paul. They give us biblical examples of how to correct our thinking if it is wrong. In my book *Living the Maximized Life.*[4] I define a maximizer as a person who possesses the strength of character that enables him to keep on believing, planning, thinking, and working to experience his full potential in the face of less than optimum conditions. It is his focused thinking, rooted in the Word of God, that gets him through.

How to Maximize the Mind

So, how do I maximize my mind? I do it when I deliberately cultivate a systematic way of thinking that keeps me on the cutting edge of life. How do I develop this systematic way of thinking?

First, *I need to believe that there's a better way of doing things.* In other words, no matter what I'm doing now or how successful I am at it, I must believe that there's a better way of doing it. I may be doing it the best I know how, but there's a

better way. Without thinking like that, we'd have no inventions—no new ideas or innovations. If man had stopped with
the calculator, we wouldn't have computers. Always thinking
that there's a better way to do what you do is the only way you
will make a demand on the potential that's inside you.

Second, *I must be able to focus intensely without distraction,* because focus will supersede intelligence any day. I told a
story at a church once about a man who had a squirrel invad-
ing his property. The man was trying to find a way to keep the
squirrel out. He went to the hardware store, bought what they
told him was an anti-squirrel contraption, took it to his house,
and set it up. The squirrel figured out how to get around it. The
man took it back to the hardware store and complained. The
sales clerk said, "Nothing has been created or invented that
will keep that squirrel off your property."

The customer said, "Wait a minute. We have the genius to
put a man on the moon, and you're telling me that we can't
keep a squirrel out?"

"No," said the clerk. "Think about it this way. How long did
you think about trying to keep that squirrel out? How much
mind power did you put on it?"

"Two or three hours," said the customer.

"And how long do you think that squirrel thought about
how to get around what you put there to keep him out? Every
waking moment!"

That squirrel was focused on his goal. Focus will outper-
form genius and intelligence every time.

When you see athletes who excel, it's because they focus. They give themselves to their profession. Do you know how Michael Jordan started out? When he was playing basketball in high school, people said he wasn't the most talented person around. Yet he became great because of his focus.

I have a number of pastor friends around the country. One of them is very talented musically. He can sing and write music. He was very busy in ministry around the country, but at the time we talked his church was not blossoming.

Then there's another pastor friend of mine. If you had talked to him before he went into the ministry, you probably would have told him, "Please don't go into ministry. Go home and get a job, brother. Don't even try." He doesn't look like a preacher. He can hardly talk. He's not very coordinated. If he walked into a room, you'd almost feel sorry for him. You probably couldn't believe that anybody would follow him. But if you went to his church, you'd say, "Wow, look what the Lord has done!" His church is doing well simply because he's not running around the country. He's focused on being a pastor, and he has a genuine love for his people.

I was sharing with the first pastor who is so talented musically. He was running here and there and doing all these things. I told him, "Hey, you need to focus. The reason your home church isn't growing is because you're not focused."

If your marriage isn't going where it needs to, maybe it's because you're not focused. Focus is a key. We'll deal with marriage in another chapter, but maybe this will set it up for you. My marriage turned around when I got focused.

The third thing I need to do to develop a systematic way of thinking is, *I must have a systematic approach to problem solving*. This diffuses the intimidation of a problem. When I have a systematic approach to solving problems, then I believe that every problem can be dealt with and solved. The problem does not intimidate me. A problem is only a wake-up call for the divine creativity that I possess. Once intimidation is taken out of problems, I'm ready for them. God has designed me to handle problems.

Most people don't understand that God didn't create the world so Adam and Eve could just sit down and eat grapes. God created man, put him in a beautiful environment, and then challenged him to make the whole earth like the garden he was in. He told Adam to replenish the earth, subdue it, and have dominion (see Gen. 1:28). God gave him a problem to solve, because only a problem would challenge him to give birth to his full potential.

Sometimes I get really busy with work. When that happens, I just rejoice and say, "Thank God I have a job!" I remember one particular time when I'd preached and I was worn out. But when I got home, I studied for another hour or so preparing for something I had to do two weeks later. I always push myself and make a demand on myself because I know there's always a better way of doing things. That's making me a better man.

One year, I took a conference we held at our church to a whole other level. I made a demand on the staff. I told them that instead of doing what we'd done for the previous eleven years, we were going to do it differently. In the past, each conference leader had been responsible for 45 minutes. Now I wanted each leader to be responsible for four hours of intense training that would capture the attention of their group. I challenged them because I know there's always a better way.

We're looking at a man and his mind. The Bible tells us what we're supposed to think about. Look at this verse in Philippians chapter 4.

Philippians 4:8

8 Finally, brethren, whatsoever things are true, whatsoever things are honest, whatsoever things are just, whatsoever things are pure, whatsoever things are lovely, whatsoever things are of good report; if there be any virtue, and if there be any praise, think on these things.

Notice that at the end of this verse it says, "Think on these things." Here are some simple strategies for developing a maximized mentality.

First, *erroneous mental conditioning must be corrected.* The way I think is either a catalyst that stimulates my creativity or a chain that confines my choices to the limitations of my experiences. My perception is my reality.

The story is told of an experiment with a fish—a pike. Pike love to eat baitfish. The people running the experiment put the pike in one side of an aquarium divided in the middle by a glass partition. Then they put baitfish on the other side of the partition. The pike tried to get to the baitfish but kept bumping his head against the glass. Eventually he became conditioned to believe that he could not get to the fish. Then the experimenters removed the partition. The baitfish were swimming all around the pike, but he died of starvation. He had been conditioned to think that he could not get to the fish, so he quit trying.

Animal trainers use the same technique with elephants. Trainers tie a rope around a baby elephant's foot and attach the rope to a stake. The baby elephant pulls and pulls trying to get free from the stake until he finally decides it's impossible. Then, even when he becomes an adult able to move big trees, he will stay bound by the rope that's tied to the stake. He could easily pull the stake out of the ground, but he's been conditioned to think that he cannot get free.

That is what happens to humans. We are conditioned to believe that we must live in the state we're in until something or somebody shakes and rocks our world.

We are conditioned to believe that our success is somebody else's responsibility. For example, you might be conditioned to believe that your success is your boss's responsibility. That is not true. His only responsibility is to pay you for the work you do. Maybe you don't want to hear that, but it's the truth. He is only responsible to pay you for productivity. That's why he hired you. He didn't hire you to be your buddy or to become your welfare provider. It is not his responsibility, or the government's, to do so. The Lord said to Joshua that if he would do what the Lord told him to do, then *Joshua* would make his own way prosperous and have good success (Josh. 1:8).

We are conditioned to think pessimistically about life and successful others. Stop criticizing successful people and quit thinking negatively about life. "But have you seen the price of gasoline?" you might say. Yes. That industry plays a game. That's all it is. The price goes up and down. People told us years ago that we would run out, but we still have it. And through it all, I'm going to keep driving. I'm still going to have enough. My God supplies my need. I'm not ever going to run out.

We are conditioned to believe that God's plan will work for somebody else, but it won't work for us. Who told us that? Where did we get that idea from? The Bible says that God is not a respecter of persons (Acts 10:34). When I see God working in another man's life, I understand that, in principle, He must work in my life too. I saw Dr. Price's success and said, "That's a principle. It'll work for me too."

Mental Choices Common to Men
Who Mentally Maximize

Let's look at some of the mental choices common to men who maximize their minds.

Maximizers choose to think correctly. We must think correctly to keep from limiting ourselves. Look at these verses in Proverbs chapter 4.

> Proverbs 4:20–22
> 20 My son, attend to my words; incline thine ear unto my sayings.
> 21 Let them not depart from thine eyes; keep them in the midst of thine heart.
> 22 For they are life unto those that find them, and health to all their flesh.

God tells you to attend to His words. You stretch your capacity when you understand that the Word of God is truth. You have to give attention to the truth. What you do today is an investment in your future. Attending to the Word of God stretches your thinking. It's an investment in you.

Correct thinking is thinking that has been renewed based on the wisdom of God's Word. Truth for me is not what I read in the newspaper. Truth for me—about my future and my destiny—is what I read in the Word of God.

Concrete Thinking

Maximizers choose to think concretely. Concrete thinking considers both the natural facts and the spiritual truths addressing the same situation, and yet stays focused in faith. For example, Abraham considered not his own body. He knew how old he was. He knew that his physical body wasn't working like it needed to in order to produce what God said would happen. He was able to look at the natural facts without letting them move him away from the spiritual promise.

In other words, you can say, "I don't have a good education. I don't even have a good job. But the Word of God says that my God supplies all my needs (Phil. 4:19). I'm blessed of the Lord. His blessing makes me rich and He adds no sorrow to it (Prov. 10:22), and I believe the Word. I don't know how God's going to do it. I don't know how He's going to pull it off. But the Word of God says that I should have abundant life and I am not going to be denied (John 10:10). I know all the things I have to over-come. I know the deck is stacked against me, but it isn't a problem. I think concretely."

I know that some people can't stand to see a black man— especially a preacher—riding in a Rolls Royce. But that's not going to stop me from enjoying the blessings of the Lord. I know there are folks who try to talk people out of coming to my church. A woman once told me, "When I came to town, I wanted to come to your church, but all the people I knew were telling me, 'Don't go over there.' I came to your church, and I enjoy it. I'm a member. I just don't understand why people were telling me not to come over here."

I'm aware of all that, but in spite of it God raised us up and we're still growing. You have to think concretely. I know I have a swagger about me, but that's because my mind is right.

Controlled Thinking

Maximizers choose to think controlled. Controlled thinking is what we just saw in Philippians 4:8. We must be selective in both our thought processes and the subject matter we choose to think on. I choose what I think on. This freedom can never be taken from me. You cannot control what I choose to think. You can restrict my freedom in many other ways, but you cannot restrict my thought life. I control what I think.

Don't let the devil manipulate your thoughts with a fiery dart. You might be sitting in a meeting and suddenly the devil shoots a dart. He shoots a thought into your mind that your wife is being unfaithful to you. If you accept that thought, you can get upset and not hear anything the speaker is saying. All you see is your wife being unfaithful. Don't let the devil play with your mind like that. Control your thinking.

God told us to think on the things listed in Philippians 4:8 because He knew the devil would try to play games with our heads. For instance, the devil will send the thought, *What if they fire me from my job? What am I going to do? Maybe they won't fire me. But maybe they will. And if they fire me, what will I do? Well, if they fire me, I don't need this job anyway!*

Maybe you let the devil play with your mind over that and then your boss sees you and says, "What is wrong with you?" And you say, "I don't need this job. I don't need you. You just take this job and shove it!" And your boss says, "Okay. Fine." He still has income, but you don't because you didn't control your thinking. Don't let the devil or other people manipulate your thinking.

Once when I was working for a company, I thought I was in line to be a supervisor, but they hired another man for the job. Everybody I worked with told me, "Man, I wouldn't take that. If I were you, I'd quit! I'd show *them.*"

I told them, "That's stupid. I have a job. I have income and I have children and bills. I'm not going to let you force me to quit or tell me that I ought to be embarrassed to stay here and work under somebody else the boss hired."

Then I went to the boss and asked him, "How come you didn't select me? I need to know. I thought I was in line for the position."

He said, "Ira, you're a good worker, but I don't need a worker for that job. I need a manager. And until you can think and operate like a manager, you're not ready to go to the next level." Then he explained it to me. He said, "You see, in this situation, you would stay here all night and get the job done. But you can't work all night all the time. You'd burn yourself out. I need a person who understands how to motivate and delegate."

All I could say was, he was right. So I went to the guy that he hired and said, "Hey, my boss told me that you've got some skills that I don't have, so, I'm going to help you be successful so you can get promoted, because I want your job. All I want you to do is teach me what you know."

He reared back in his seat and looked up at me, because he was intimidated. He thought I was going to act like a fool and try to make him look bad. But when he found out that I wanted to be his partner, guess what happened? He trained me and showed me what he knew. In short order, I had the job. I didn't let others manipulate my mind.

Critical Thinking

Maximizers choose to think critically. Critical thinkers see beyond the moment. They carefully judge thoughts, ideas, and premonitions by the Word of God, and they apply the wisdom of that Word. They consider cause and effect, and after they have evaluated a situation, they establish a firm resolve to go in a certain direction. Behind every mishap and mistake is an inaccurate, unfounded assumption. An assumption is the lowest form of knowledge. Why assume when you can get the truth?

Creative Thinking

Maximizers choose to think creatively. Creative thinkers see new realities unvisualized by others. Creative thinking incubates solutions for problems and brings innovation to the status quo. It steps boldly outside the box of restrictive thinking to think what others will not think. Creative thinkers ask, "What if?" and chase the answer in the arena of their thought life. Creative thinking gives birth to inventions, songs, music, and art. Creative thinkers research the approaches others have used to solve problems similar to the one they face, and they adapt those solutions to their situation.

Courageous Thinking

Maximizers choose to think courageously. Courageous thinking distinguishes us from the crowd. When others think and talk, courageous thinkers think and act. They are willing to step outside the norm. They are willing to continue to perform under extreme pressure, because they have a warrior's mentality. I don't mean that a courageous thinker gets into a physical fight. I mean that he's a thinker. He has yielded his mind to the Spirit of God, and he understands that for every problem, there is a divine solution. Courageous thinkers maintain a faith focus under great pressure. Despite what things look like, they keep on believing.

I'm willing to yield myself to the Spirit of God because He will guide me into the company of the people I need to know. He will see that I have the knowledge I need that is critical to my success and my destiny in life. My thinking is uncluttered, so I can think creatively. I can do all things through Christ which strengthens me. When I encounter a problem, I get excited, because that means I'm going to another level.

I remember one problem we had when we were putting up a building. We'd poured the piers, but it was raining so much that we couldn't lay the foundation, and we were running out of time for what we wanted to do.

As we thought about it, we realized that the building was not going to sit on the foundation; it was going to sit on the piers, beams and all, so we decided to be innovative. Before we laid the floor, we put up the frame of the building and closed it in. The roof kept the rain off, and we came in and laid the floors. We thought creatively. Whatever problem you're facing, you have the creativity inside you to handle it. God engineered you that way.

Use Your Creativity

You might think that I'm really smart to have thought of that with the building project. But I'm not talking just about me. You're smart too. The only difference between you and me is, I woke up my creativity. I run after a problem, like David did when he saw Goliath. Everybody else was thinking about fighting Goliath in hand-to-hand combat. But David thought, *I need a missile to take that man down. A missile will give me the advantage.* The rest of the Israelite army was thinking the way Goliath wanted them to think, but David got a rock, put it in a sling, and hurled it while he was still some distance from the man. David knocked him down, picked up Goliath's sword, and chopped his head off. David was a thinker.

What Goliath is intimidating you and causing you to shake in your boots? What situation is keeping you up at night? Whatever it is, there's divine creativity inside you to handle that problem and chart new paths. Don't worry if folks talk about you. Creative thinkers are always talked about. They always have rocks thrown at them, but don't pick up the rocks and throw them back. You don't have time for that. Take the rocks people throw at you and use them to build paths for them to follow, because what is criticized today will be applauded tomorrow.

11

A Man and
His Marriage

The objective of this chapter is to give some clarity to God's plan for marriage. We'll look at marriage from a Biblical perspective. Every married Christian man must resolve to honor God in his marriage commitment in order to strengthen the testimony of marriage in our generation and for the generations to come.

Let's look first at passage of Scripture in Ephesians chapter 5 that deals with marriage.

Ephesians 5:21–25

21 Submitting yourselves one to another in the fear of God.

22 Wives, submit yourselves unto your own husbands, as unto the Lord.

23 For the husband is the head of the wife, even as Christ is the head of the church: and he is the saviour of the body.

24 Therefore as the church is subject unto Christ, so let the wives be to their own husbands in every thing.

25 Husbands, love your wives, even as Christ also loved the church, and gave himself for it.

Notice in verse 25 that husbands are to give themselves up for their wives just as Christ gave himself for the Church. Jesus gave up His comfort and what He wanted for our sake. And we husbands are to do the same for our wives.

Now here's my working definition for marriage.

Marriage is a divine institution established by God and entered into by two free moral agents of the opposite sex who enter into covenant with each other and with God to live together for the rest of their lives with another imperfect person in a manner which glorifies God.

When I'm getting ready to get married, I say to God, "I realize that I'm imperfect and my future wife is imperfect. But we're going to covenant to live together for the rest of our lives, and we're going to have to deal with each other's imperfections."

The strength of a marriage is determined by the capacity and willingness of the partners to manage the imperfections that surface throughout the relationship. It's a growing thing. Here is something else the Scriptures have to say about marriage.

Colossians 3:18–19
18 Wives, submit yourselves unto your own husbands, as it is fit in the Lord.
19 Husbands, love your wives, and be not bitter against them.

It's the husband's job not to be harsh, bitter, or resentful toward his wife, but to be affectionate and sympathetic. As stated in 1 Peter 3:7, husbands are to live considerately with [your wives], with an intelligent recognition [of the marriage relationship], honoring the woman as [physically] the weaker, but [realizing that you] are joint heirs of the grace (God's unmerited favor) of life, in order that your prayers may not be hindered and cut off. {Otherwise you cannot pray effectively.}. That's the will of God.

Obstacles to God's Plan for Marriage

So, how do I make a marriage work? There are five obstacles that must be overcome to usher in God's will for your marriage. The first one is *ignorance of God's order for marriage*. Most people were not taught about marriage and they don't have a clear understanding of how God views this institution. The second one is *adoption of the world's perception of marriage*. Your view of the world's perception of marriage will be based on the world you grew up in. If you grew up around old-school thinking, then you believe that when you tell your wife something, she'd better do it. But if you do that today, you might find out that your wife doesn't need you. The rules have changed. What once was, is no more. What defined manhood in a wife's eyes in earlier times does not define manhood now. God's rules for manhood have never changed, but people have not adopted them.

The third obstacle to be overcome is *a hidden, premarital, selfish agenda*. Why did we get married? That's the question. Most of us get married for selfish reasons. Can we admit that? We got married because we had a selfish agenda. It was about what we thought she could do for us and mean for us. Our marriages won't get better until we admit that and grow beyond selfishness.

I married my wife because I needed a wife in order to have a big church, and I wanted a big church. And she was pretty. I didn't want an ugly girl. I know some guys like ugly girls. I don't. And she was well connected in the church world. Her daddy was chairman of a deacon board. I was a young preacher and I needed a wife, because in those days when you preached at churches to try out for a pastorate, if you didn't have a wife, they didn't want to hire you. They wouldn't even give you a shot at the church. They wanted you to be settled. I had to get settled to qualify, so I married a nice little church girl.

It would have been better if she could've played the organ or sung. That could have helped me. Churches like that. She didn't have those qualities, but her daddy was chairman of a deacon board. Many times, it helps to be connected right. If you were trying out for one church, the chairman of that deacon board would call the chairman of another deacon board and ask about you. The deacon board chairmen talk with each other at conventions. I figured it wouldn't be too bad to be married to the daughter of a deacon board chairman.

But things didn't work out. I didn't get the church. So guess who I blamed? Her. It was all her fault, I decided. Then, all her deficits starting looking bigger. I'd tell her, "You can't play. You can't sing. I don't know what I need you for." I was being selfish. The only thing that kept us married was that I knew I had made a commitment to God and to her.

Now I'd been married before, but the first time around I was just an immature kid. I didn't know any better. This time, though, I was mature. I knew what I was doing. I was still selfish, but I knew I'd made a covenant with God, and I wasn't going to back off of that.

I went from preacher to preacher asking how to have a good marriage, but I didn't know anybody who was happily married. In fact, I knew a preacher's son who was getting ready to marry about then. Bridget and I were having all kinds of problems. He knew his daddy was talking to us, and everybody knew we were having problems. This guy was getting cold feet a couple of weeks before the wedding. He was a preacher's son marrying a preacher's daughter. He told me, "Hilliard, I don't know anybody who's happily married." He knew his parents were not. He knew the parents of the girl he was marrying were not. I couldn't tell him I was. And I couldn't tell him about any other couples, because nobody I knew was happily married.

I said, "That's a shame." Then I decided that wasn't going to happen to me. I decided that I was going to be a happily married preacher. I said to God, "If you show me how to have a happy marriage, I'll show everybody else." And He showed me.

The fourth obstacle that must be overcome to usher in God's will for marriage is *the common confusion between love and romance.* And the fifth obstacle is *the mishandling of mistakes, errors, and misguided expectations.*

What Happened When I Said, 'I Do'?

So, what happened when I said, "I do," and I stepped into marriage? Here are five things that took place.

1. I stepped into a divine role that provided fulfillment at a new level.

2. I began to experience the favor of God reserved only for that state. Proverbs 18:22 says, "Whoso findeth a wife

findeth a good thing, and obtaineth favour of the Lord." There's favor from God at that level that an unmarried man cannot experience.

3. I took on God's plan to live for the benefit of another. That's the key. In marriage, I live for the benefit of another person. Until I see marriage that way, I'll hold on to my selfish agenda and I will always be disappointed.

4. I became responsible to God and my generation for the testimony of marriage. That young preacher's son told me he didn't know anybody who was happily married. That was because the people he was looking at had failed to properly represent the testimony of marriage in their generation. Folks won't read the Bible, but they'll look at your life and marriage. When they do, they ought to be encouraged and want to be married too.

5. I secretly brought into another person's life all of my emotional baggage and deficits. When I married, I brought all the emotional garbage—all my past disap-pointments, hurts, and abuses—into that relationship. I didn't do it intentionally. I wasn't trying to harm my spouse, but if I don't correct the problems, then I will be punishing my wife for something somebody else did.

When my first marriage broke up, my ex-wife got the house. It wasn't a mansion, but we'd owned it. I'm not putting my first wife down. We were both young and foolish, and I take full responsibility for my part. But I left that relationship saying, "If I remarry, that isn't going to happen again. I'm not buying a house. We're going to rent." That was baggage. After

Bridget and I married, it was a long time before we bought a house. We rented.

That attitude was garbage from the past, and garbage smells bad. During the courtship, you know, you perfumed that thing down. You were on your best behavior. You opened the door for her when she got into the car. You were at your best.

But remember, your wife brought garbage into the relationship too. She brought all her hurts and pain and abuses, and she perfumed down her garbage too. She acted really nice. You went hiking and she told you she liked the outdoors, so you planned on going camping after you married. Then after the wedding she said, "I'm not going out in the woods with you." You said, "Wait a minute, baby. Didn't we go hiking when we were courting?" She said, "Yeah, but I did that just to make you happy."

So if you can picture this, at the wedding you had two folks standing at the altar, and over their shoulders were bags of stinky, smelly garbage that they had perfumed down. My point is, during the courtship we perfume down all the garbage from our past. You might even see some trash, but you overlook it. But once you're married and you go home after the honeymoon, you open up those bags and they start stinking. Reality settles in. You wake up and see her without makeup. She wakes up and finds out there are little nubs growing out of your face that stick her when you try to kiss her. Before, she always saw you clean-shaven.

How to Strengthen a Relationship

So, how can I strengthen my marriage relationship? The story about Jesus turning water into wine in John 2:1–11 is good to use when looking at how to transform a marriage. It shows us that with Him in the picture, things can change.

I need to remember that God tells me to love my wife as Jesus loved the Church (Eph. 5:25). Now, I have a question: when has the Church ever done everything Jesus asked it to do? It never has. So when God tells you to love your wife even as Jesus loved the Church, He's saying, "Even if she doesn't do what you ask her to do, you have to love her anyway." Real men love their wives that way.

To bring change to a marriage, a man has to face whatever erroneous reason he had for marrying. He can't cover them up. He has to deal with them. Here are some wrong reasons people use to marry:

- To please parents or escape parental control.
- To have children in an acceptable way.
- To provide a father or mother for existing children.
- To get back at a former mate or lover.
- To enhance a career with the appearance of stability.
- To have readily available sex, or sex upon demand.
- To have a comfortable lifestyle. Living on two incomes is better than living on one.

Whatever wrong reasons I may have had to marry, I have to identify them and deal with them.

Dealing With Incompatibility

To strengthen my marriage, I must identify and deal with areas of incompatibility. *Incompatibility* is the state of being incapable of peaceful association because of incongruity, disagreement, and discord. In other words, we disagree and have trouble getting along in certain areas. We have to identify these areas. Let's look at six major areas of incompatibility.

1. Communication. There might be an inability to intellectually discuss and resolve issues. Wives want their husbands to talk to them. One of the major complaints wives in our church share with my wife is, "He won't talk. He just sits there and looks at the TV." Maybe you used to talk, but too often you got criticized or she didn't listen to you. So you stopped talking. You don't want to be bothered. But remember, you're a thinking man, and a thinking man gets creative and overcomes.

You have to talk to your wife. She needs a man to talk to her, and she'll find another one to do it if you won't. I don't mean she'll be unfaithful, but she'll find another man to talk to her. I always encourage men to have a day of talking. My wife and I call it a "family meeting." We just sit down and talk. Your wife likes to hear you talk. She wants you to talk to her. She wants to hear what's on your mind.

2. Finances. Maybe you and your wife disagree over values and money-management goals. Whichever partner has the best mind for money ought to be the one managing the money. In my house, I'm not the one. I hate details—I have too many other things to do. My gift is making money. I was doing that before I became a pastor. I bought my wife a car for her wedding gift. Making money was never a problem for me, once

I learned how to do it. But I tell my wife, "I make the money. You spend it." And we agreed that we would save a certain percentage of our income and pay the bills on time.

3. Spiritual matters. Maybe there is discord in your home in the application of righteous principles. If you're going to the right church, and you're both going to the same church, you should be able to get into agreement on spiritual issues. If you come to the church I pastor, all you have to do is sit down and talk to one of the associate pastors. He'll help you get into spiritual agreement based on the Word of God.

4. Sexual matters. Maybe there are unresolved attempts at sexual fulfillment in your relationship. You and your wife need to get together and talk about sex. Of course, you can't expect your wife to do things to satisfy your sexual appetite if that appetite is perverted and not in line with the Word of God. The Bible has some criteria for sexual relations. Some people carry that too far, but the Scriptures do have some standards. Those criteria, along with the witness of the hearts of the partners, define what you can do sexually.

5. Career matters. There might be disagreements over career pursuits within the relationship.

6. Recreational matters. Maybe you and your spouse can't agree over what activities to pursue together. You ought to enjoy marriage and each other. I don't know why folks get married and quit having fun. When was the last time you just had some fun with your wife? You get on the treadmill of going to work, coming home, eating, sleeping, getting up, and going to work the next day. Marriage ought to be fun. Your wife didn't marry you for you to become a couch potato. You have to learn how to have fun.

Maybe you're saying, "If we had more money, we could have some fun." You can have fun without a lot of money. Your wife just wants to be with you. My wife and I used to go and just get ice cream. I'd get a Coke float with two scoops, until I could afford three. Before we could take elaborate vacations, we'd just drive from Houston to Galveston. We'd talk on the way down, find a place that sold ice cream, eat a little, walk along the beach, turn around, and come back.

We need to address these six areas of incompatibility. You and your wife need to deal with any of these that are a problem, because if you don't, they will always be a thorn in your flesh. Once you get into agreement, God's power is there to help you. Bridget and I found out that it was economically damaging for us to be out of agreement. The Scriptures say, "If two of you shall agree on earth as touching any thing that they shall ask, it shall be done for them of my Father which is in heaven" (Matt. 18:19).

My wife and I value agreement, and agreement doesn't necessarily mean that I like it. It means that I have submitted myself to handling something a certain way. I don't argue and have an attitude about it. If we agree we're going to do something a certain way, then we'll do it that way.

Commitments to Maintain Compatibility

Now we're going to look at twelve commitments we need to make that are essential to establishing and maintaining compatibility in a marriage. Your mate is a reflection of your intelligent choice. Like it or not, each time you look at your mate, you see a reflection of your intelligence. When you go home and look at your wife, you need to remember that you chose her, and your choice reflects your intelligence.

So here are twelve commitments that husbands and wives need to make to remain compatible.

- *Commit to being anchored in the Word.* Both partners must do this. That will give you a common value system. If you want to get your marriage in order, especially in the Body of Christ, you must be anchored in the Word.

- *Commit to unconditional love.* That means I'm going to love my spouse as unto the Lord. I'm going to keep my relationship with Him strong, and my wife will get the overflow of that relationship. When I do that, then when I love her, I'm not expecting anything in return. I'm going to treat my wife the way God wants me to treat her whether she acts right or not. That was the covenant I made when I decided that I was no longer going to look for what she could do for me. I decided to treat her the way God wants me to, regardless of what she did.

- *Commit to protect the relationship from competing affections.* You must establish guidelines to do this. In other words, I must not let any other relationship compete with my marriage. I must not get involved in anything that will draw me away from my relationship with my wife.

Each year, the very first thing I do when I'm planning my calendar is to put down my vacation time with my wife. People are always pulling at me wanting me to do things. You can't do everything for everybody, but quality time with my wife comes first. I began doing that years ago when our church first started, because my mentor told me to do that. I protect my relationship with my wife. The men in the church I pastor wouldn't respect me if I told them how to take care of their marriages when mine wasn't right.

- *Commit to establish a consistent communication forum.* Plan a family meeting, a scheduled time to talk. Most couples don't do this, but having a set time to talk will take away so much tension from your relationship. Set a time to talk every Friday or Saturday or whatever day works for you. I call it the family meeting. You may not need it, but your wife does.

- *Commit to submit to an accountable entity or individual.* In other words, if you're having trouble, you both need to submit your disagreement to someone else to whom you can be accountable. You need that accountability.

- *Commit to have the maturity to make corporate decisions, and resolve to stay focused.* In other words, you and your wife decide that you will not make certain purchases unless you're in agreement. You each may have a credit card with plenty of room on it. But you've said to each other that you won't buy anything that costs more than a certain amount unless you both agree. And you need to be sensitive enough to know when your wife says yes but her heart is not in it. You need to consider what she likes and wants.

Years ago a guy going to our church heard about how God wants us to prosper, and he bought himself a two-seater convertible as the family car. I think he had about five children. His wife complained, and I talked to him about it. He said, "I work hard for my money. It's time for me to have a car like that." I told him, "No, it isn't time, brother. Now, it may be time after all those children are grown up and out of the house. Maybe then you can go get a car like that for you and momma. But right now, how are you going to get everybody where they need to go? You'll have to make two or three trips just to get to church!"

- *Commit to accept godly council and wisdom to mediate differences.*

- *Commit to maintain self-worth and self-esteem based on God, apart from your mate.* In other words, it would be good if my wife could affirm me and esteem me, but if she hasn't grown to that point, then I need to get my affirmation from my relationship with God, not from a woman. If my wife isn't affirming me, then I must not fall into the trap of wanting to hear another woman tell me how wonderful I am.

- *Commit to establish a proven, problem-solving regimen.* That will eliminate feeling overwhelmed by problems.

- *Commit to stay in an atmosphere of faith that supports marriage.* In other words, don't take your family out of a church that believes in marriage and families.

- *Commit to avoid jealousy and competition with other married couples.* Rejoice with other couples when they are blessed, but don't feel like you have to match them and beat them. Maybe a husband you know bought his wife an expensive diamond ring, and your wife sees it. Or maybe a husband you know bought a fancy pickup truck, and his wife is glad he has it. As a couple, you have to commit that you won't let yourselves get jealous of another couple's blessings. Don't let yourselves compete and get into a financial strain.

- *Commit to always keep your word and respect the rights of your mate.* Always keep your word. Don't lie. Trust is hard to build and easy to destroy. It may take a lifetime to build it back. Always trust your mate.

Promises Honorable Men Make to Their Wives

There are four things that every man of honor should promise to do for his spouse: pray for her, partner with her, push her, and be passionate toward her.

1. Pray for your spouse. This is one thing I love to do. At night when I'm in bed with my wife, I put my arm around her, and then I pray for her.

2. Partner with your spouse. She's my partner. She's not my competitor. She adds to my life; she doesn't take away from it.

3. Push your spouse. In other words, you may see potential in her that she doesn't see in herself. Encourage her in that area.

4. Be passionate toward your spouse. Show her in meaningful ways that you love her. Our wives need our love. They shouldn't need to look anywhere else for it. Real men love their wives.

12

A Man and
His Mantle

In this chapter, we're attempting to cause you as a man to think about and be responsible for future generations. We're doing this so that we don't just live our lives focused on what we have today. We need to understand that real men provide for the future…the future of the Kingdom of God and the future of their families. This chapter is about leaving a legacy for future generations. We use the symbol of a mantle because when Elijah went to be with the Lord, he left his mantle behind, and Elisha picked it up and used it in his ministry. So a mantle is symbolic of leaving a legacy, a pattern of success, something that is laid up so that future generations can profit from our having been here.

Let's look at some scripture that relates to this topic.

Proverbs 13:22
A good man leaveth an inheritance to his children's children:
and the wealth of the sinner is laid up for the just.

Joshua 24:14-15

14 Now therefore fear the LORD, and serve him in sincerity and in truth: and put away the gods which your fathers served on the other side of the flood, and in Egypt; and serve ye the LORD.

15 And if it seem evil unto you to serve the LORD, choose you this day whom ye will serve; whether the gods which your fathers served that were on the other side of the flood, or the gods of the Amorites, in whose land ye dwell: but as for me and my house, we will serve the LORD.

The promise of manhood fathering for future generational blessing is in the Bible. Generational blessing is the favor of God available to a generation which was acquired by previous generations through obedience to God, offerings to God, or the oracles of God.

Scripture shows that those who honored God accrued generational favor for their families. When God gave a promise, He gave it not just to one man but also to his lineage, his descendants. The Bible says God made the promise to Abraham, but it was also to his seed (Gen. 22:15–18, 26:24; Gal. 3:16). God made a promise to David, but he really made it to David and his seed (2 Sam. 7:12–16). God made a promise to mankind and he told him to be fruitful and multiply (Gen. 1:26–28, 9:1–17). The promise had generational implications. So we see that when God talks to a man, he's not just talking to him. He's talking to the generations that will come out of him.

What I Do Affects Others

So our thinking has to change. We need to know that what we do affects others. We need to live as responsible men. When we understand this responsibility, it causes us to restrict and curtail some of our present activity.

For example, I used to smoke a pipe. I did it to be cool. Then one day my daughter asked me, "Daddy can I do that?"

"No, you can't do it."

"Well, why are you doing it?"

That ended my day. I could not give her a reason why it was okay for me and wasn't okay for her. I could have said, "I'm grown, and you're not." But I didn't. I gave away the whole pipe collection. I realized I could have been contributing to her delinquency by her seeing me involved in behavior that would not be good for her.

Generational Consciousness

I have to have a generational consciousness. It is a major dysfunction when a generation chooses to abdicate its responsibility to work toward the advancement of the next generation.

Now you can be conscious of different things as you live your life. You can live your life based on what I call a gain consciousness, that is, my value is based upon what I possess, or, I can live my life based on greed consciousness. Here, my value is based on selfish surplus. Or I can live based on God consciousness. In other words, my value comes from my relationship with God. But God wants me to rise to a place of generational conscious, where my value is based on my mentoring and the inheritance I leave.

Generational consciousness causes me to understand that I am responsible for the success of the next generation. I cannot live my life as though I don't have that responsibility.

The people of the civil rights movement, both black and white, gave their blood and themselves so that my generation could have what it has. Many of those people never saw or experienced the things they fought for, but they had a generational consciousness.

Today we're losing that consciousness. We've reached the land of plenty and we have forgotten our responsibility to provide for the next generation. I don't just mean providing money. I mean providing moral fortitude and a consciousness of God. The reason we spend the money we do on our children is to give them a God-consciousness. The world is doing everything it can to eradicate God-consciousness from them, and if we don't invest in them, they won't have it. We have to think generationally.

At our church, we spent a lot of money on children's facilities. We were investing in a God-consciousness for those children. If you don't get them when they are children, it's hard to get them when they are teens, and almost impossible to get them after that. Real men leave an inheritance for their children's children.

We Need a Multigenerational Vision

I have to develop a vision that is multigenerational. If I don't have that, I live life only for myself. I must understand the responsibility of the parental state. Many men are parents and are not married, or they are parents who are not with some of their biological children. But being in those conditions does not remove their responsibility. A man cannot let anger at his mate cause him not to take care of his children.

Today, the laws of the land are very protective of children, and we praise God for that. The law will make you pay for the care of your children. But if you are sitting in church under the Word of God, nobody should have to make you take care of your children. Real men pay their child support, because real men obey the law. It's important in God's eyes to do that, because for one thing, it gives the children a righteous example. Look at this verse from the Book of Proverbs.

> Proverbs 22:6
> 6 Train up a child in the way he should go: and when he is old, he will not depart from it.

The goal of the parental state is not to raise a perfect, mistake-free person. It is to oversee the development of a well-balanced individual who is capable of responding to life's challenges in a manner that glorifies God. To do that, we must do at least three things.

1. *We must guide our children through the precepts and principles of God's Word.* That's why it's important to get them into a good church and to live your own life by God's principles. Even though many times they act like they're not listening to you, they're really listening to every word you say.

2. *We must guard our children and protect them from the wiles of the devil who seeks to destroy them through*

wicked and unrighteous influences. It's our responsibility as their parents to guard them.

3. *We must remember that God's grace is all-sufficient for the child or children entrusted to our care.*

The Bible says that my children are an inheritance from the Lord. We see this in Psalm 127.

Psalm 127:3–4

3 Lo, children are an heritage of the LORD: and the fruit of the womb is his reward.

4 As arrows are in the hand of a mighty man; so are children of the youth.

Verse 4 compares my children to arrows in my hand, so I must be able to evaluate my children and properly direct their lives. It's my responsibility to point them in the right direction. And if I'm really smart, I'll build a team with my children. I've mentored my own children and built a team, and my children are involved in ministry.

I don't know why it is, but many men see parenting as a woman's job. It's not a woman's job, even though many women may take a major role in it. Part of our responsibility as men is to train our children.

Challenges to Parents

There are challenges in the parental state. When we look at our children, there are four types of child we have to deal with. There's *the unwanted child,* the one you had when you were just having fun. But that child is still yours. Then there's *the special needs child*—one who needs extra attention to develop properly. This child may be physically deformed or may have some level of retardation. But the child is still yours, and he or she needs special attention in order to develop. Then there's *the rebellious child*—the child who causes sorrow. That child you pray for, and if they become toxic you have to deal with them at a whole other level. Most people don't have the strength to do that. When you read in the paper that a child killed his parents, you know that there was a toxic child situation that was not dealt with properly.

Then there's *the obedient child.* Just because a child is obedient doesn't mean that child should not be rewarded. We tend to give more attention to a disobedient child and think an obedient child will be all right. Everybody applauds the Prodigal Son's father, but I submit to you that he had a real dysfunction in his own life. We applaud him for receiving the young boy back, but when the older boy said, "Hey, Daddy, you never threw a party for me," the father told him, "Go throw your own party." You probably never looked at the story like that. The older son said, "Daddy, I stayed here with you. I've been the obedient son, and you've never thrown me a party." And all his daddy could tell him was, "The whole place is yours. You could have given yourself a party." An obedient child should be affirmed too.

Children are going to fall into one of those four categories: the unwanted child, the rebellious child, the special needs child, and the obedient child. But they all need me, and there is a level of spiritual responsibility I have toward each one.

When it comes to the rebellious child—and the Prodigal Son is an example of that kind of child—his father didn't run after him when he left. Many times, the hog pen can teach a lesson that wisdom which is not received can't teach. Sometimes children will accept a lesson that the hog pen teaches that they would not accept from you when you were trying to give them wisdom. Many times, you cannot rescue children from the consequences of their disobedience.

Levels of Spiritual Parenting

There are four levels of spiritual parenting. First, there is *infancy.* That's when I nurture, guard, and protect a child. In infancy, a child can't do anything but eat. The child cannot protect himself. It's your responsibility to nurture and protect him.

The second stage of parenting is *childhood.* This is a time of training, teaching, and being patient with the child. Then comes *adolescence.* That is a time for instruction and discipline. You discipline them in that which you've taught them while others are trying to get what you've taught them out of them. And because God made us with a spirit of independence, teenagers reach a stage where they'll listen to others before they will listen to you.

Then there's *adulthood*—a time of guidance and wisdom that produces responsible living. And when your children become adults, you have to let them be adults. You can't run their lives.

Instructions for Godly Parenting

The Bible instructs us to do ten things as godly parents. We can extract these principles from how God dealt with Adam and Eve in the Book of Genesis. It is our responsibility as parents to do these things for our children.

1. *God organized Adam's world before He brought him into it* (Gen. 1:1–25). You should not have a child until you yourself are organized and you're ready to have a child.

2. *God made sufficient provision for His child's complete growth* (Gen. 2:15–16). God created everything Adam needed before he brought Adam on the scene.

3. *God took personal responsibly for His child* (Gen. 2:7–8, 3:21). God had a home prepared for Adam and everything he needed to function was there. Even when Adam sinned, God made provision for him.

4. *God became the model of excellence for His child* (Gen. 1:26). God became Adam's example because of the environment that He put him in and because He created him in His image.

5. *God instructed Adam in principles for successful living* (Gen. 1:29). You are responsible to teach your children how to succeed. I always saw my family as a team, so as my children grew up, I spoke to them that they were to work with us in ministry. I started telling them that when they were little, and they grew up hearing it. I am so fulfilled as a father now, because my kids work in ministry.

Teach your children team concepts—how the family can work together as a team for success. This will help the kids not to just grow up and go their separate ways without interacting with each other. They may have different professions, but they'll know that a family should work together as a team, because they can accomplish more together than as individuals.

6. *God established guidelines for righteousness for Adam* (Gen. 2:15–17). God didn't just put him in the garden. He gave him instructions. He said, "You can eat of every tree but that one." He told Adam clearly what to do.

7. *God respected His child's right to make choices and experience the consequences.* In other words, when God saw Adam choose to go against His order, God respected His child's right to choose. And with us, even when our children are adults, we must respect their right to do what they want to do. We can tell them, "You don't need that kind of car right now," but if they want it anyway, fine. When they come back later and say, "I didn't know the insurance was going to be that high," then they are experiencing a consequence of their right to choose.

8. *God instructed Adam in proper stewardship* (Gen. 2:15). He told him to dress the garden and keep it.

9. *God allowed His child to experience the negative consequences of his poor choices* (Gen. 3:6–19). When Adam and Eve sinned, God didn't shield them from the experience that followed as a result of their choices. They had to go through something.

10. *God provided a clear plan for His child's restoration in an atmosphere of faith* (Gen. 3:15,21). He helped Adam

when he made a negative choice. He gave him a plan of restoration. We owe our children that. Some children may not receive it. If they don't, then until they decide to repent and be restored God's way, all we can do is pray for them.

What I really want you to see is that we need a generational consciousness, because what we do affects future generations. Every man ought to have life insurance. You can leave a million-dollar estate by having a million dollars worth of life insurance. Your children shouldn't have to struggle like you struggled. And if you have instructed them properly, they'll know how to handle a million dollars. Remember, the Bible tells me to leave an inheritance not just for my children, but for my children's children.

I bought some land but it's not for me or my children. It's for my children's children. I don't plan to sell it, because God isn't making any more land. It's just part of my estate. I'm doing it because my children and my children's children shouldn't have to start where I started. They should have an advantage in life. They shouldn't have to start at the bottom.

You need to spend time with your children, even when they've become adults, to keep that cohesiveness of family. Don't let them scatter and go their separate ways. It's important for them to understand the power of family.

Culturally, we as black people have not valued family because a game was played with our minds when our ancestors were brought here in slavery. In those days, a man would not unite with his family because he knew that his family would be torn apart. He was seen as nothing more than a stud used to produce offspring. If we don't watch it, that mentality will perpetuate itself generation after generation. But as men of God, whatever our color, we have the truth of God's Word and we understand that we're supposed to build families that will glorify God. In other words, all the advances we make in the Kingdom of God should not go down the drain when we die.

Our church in Houston is starting a vocational college so we can train the next generation. And I'm taking the time to mentor my children and any other child who wants to be mentored, because it is time for us to be conscious of future generations. It has been said that there's no true success without a successor. I tell every manager and supervisor on the church staff that they have to train a successor who can do what they do. Whatever your position, if you haven't trained anybody to do what you do, then you are not a success.

Teach your kids what you know. Spend time with them. I love business, so I taught all my children business. When they were little, I put them into business making cuff links and selling them to preacher friends of mine. I think we called the business A Cuff Above. I'd buy them little stones for the cuff links and show them how to put them together. They'd assemble them, put them in boxes, and sell them. Those kids had a system. They even got the baby girl involved. She'd put the cuff links into the boxes. I'd call my preacher friends and say, "You'd better buy some cuff links."

I wore those cuff links too. When a pair would break, the kids would say, "Well, Daddy probably broke them himself." But I'd tell them, "No. Daddy's your customer. You need to go out of your way to make him happy. Get those broken cuff links back from him and give him another set." I was teaching them how to run a business.

When our church was getting ready to buy the former Lakewood Church facility, one of my daughters worked with one of our pastors to put together the whole loan package. When we bought a hangar for our aircraft, another one of my daughters put that project together. I told them, "I taught you business, and I'm going to watch how you handle it. You have to call the banker and take care of the other details." When they made mistakes such as not following through, they heard about it. Why? Because I'm conscious of future generations, and I want them to know more than I know and be able to do more than I do. I sit back and watch them work. It's fulfilling, but you have to take the time to do it.

So in your own life, don't just put food on the table and send your kids off to school. They need your mentoring. They need you to teach them how to work together and build a legacy and wealth as a family.

One day I was talking to another minister who has a television program, and I told him that I'd seen his son on the program and he was doing a good job. The other minister told me, "Yeah, he's my social security." What he meant was, "I'm investing in him because in my latter days I will be depending on him." That's how you ought to bring up your children. You ought to be investing in them, because in your later years you're going to be depending on them.

Your children are the arrows in your hand, and what happens in your future is up to you. You're making your future now, based on how you're dealing with your children. My wife and I took care of my mother in her latter days. She lived with us. We chose to do that, and it wasn't a problem, because my mother taught me to take care of her. When my sister and I were little children, she'd give us money on Mother's Day and tell us to go to the store and buy her a gift. She was teaching us that on special days, Mamma gets a gift. I did it for years, and when I became an adult I was trained to get Mamma a gift on Mother's Day and her birthday. She also taught us that she was our responsibility when she could not take care of herself. After my father died, Mamma could no longer live in their home. My sister and I talked it over. My wife and I were better off financially than my sister, and we were getting ready to build a house. I talked to my wife about adding a room for Mamma. My wife agreed, and we were able to do that.

But our taking care of my mother didn't just happen. I was trained to do it. And you have to train your children to respect you and that you are their responsibility. You do not want to get old and then try to tell them what they ought to do for you. How are they going to know if you didn't tell them?

So it is important that we develop a generational consciousness. Real men don't just live for today. Real men provide for the future of the Kingdom of God, and they provide for the future of their families. We need to leave our mantle— our legacy, our pattern of success—so that future generations will be better off because we were here.

Endnotes

[1] *Webster's New World College Dictionary,* Third Ed. (New York: Simon & Schuster Macmillan, 1996), 934.

[2] *Mental Toughness for Success,* (Houston: Light Publications, 1999). www.newlight.org

[3] http://www.merriam-webster.com/dictionary/meditate.

[4] *Living the Maximized Life,* (Houston: Light Publications, 2006). www.newlight.org

Prayer of Salvation

God loves you—no matter who you are, no matter what your past. God loves you so much that He gave His one and only begotten Son for you. The Bible tells us that "...whoever believes in him shall not perish but have eternal life" (John 3:16 NIV). Jesus laid down His life and rose again so that we could spend eternity with Him in heaven and experience His absolute best on earth. If you would like to receive Jesus into your life, say the following prayer out loud and mean it from your heart.

> *Heavenly Father, I come to You admitting that I am a sinner. Right now, I choose to turn away from sin, and I ask You to cleanse me of all unrighteousness. I believe that Your Son, Jesus, died on the cross to take away my sins. I also believe that He rose again from the dead so that I might be forgiven of my sins and made righteous through faith in Him. I call upon the name of Jesus Christ to be the Savior and Lord of my life. Jesus, I choose to follow You and ask that You fill me with the power of the Holy Spirit. I declare that right now I am a child of God. I am free from sin and full of the righteousness of God. I am saved in Jesus' name. Amen.*

If you prayed this prayer to receive Jesus Christ as your Savior for the first time, please contact us on the web at **www.harrisonhouse.com** to receive a free book.

Or you may write to us at
Harrison House
P.O. Box 35035
Tulsa, Oklahoma 74153

About the Author

Ira V. Hilliard, a native Houstonian, was called at the age of nine to preach God's Word.

He married the beautiful Bridget E. Harrison on October 4, 1975.

Drs. I. V. and Bridget Hilliard are the co-founders of the dynamic New Light Christian Center Church ("One Church, Multiple locations") in North and South Houston, Beaumont and Austin, Texas and the most recently acquired East Houston Campus (formerly Lakewood Church—Northeast Campus). Their passion to take God's Word to a hurting and lost generation has resulted in a current membership of over 28,000 and counting.

In addition to the awesome teaching they provide through New Light Christian Center Church's nationwide television ministry, Drs Hilliard also established a drug rehabilitation center for men and women (Life Change Institute), the ministry's own satellite network, an Aviation Division, and Early Childhood Development Centers.

Dr. Hilliard has been recognized for various scholarly honors and has written several life-changing books, which include *Mental Toughness for Success, Victory Over Stress*, and *10 Mistakes Most Failures Make and How to Avoid Them*. Most recently, Dr. Hilliard accepted an opportunity to write for Nelson Publishers after being approached by them, resulting in the release of his current best seller, *Living the Maximized Life*.

With a staff of 260 people to assist them, Drs. Hilliard have committed to creating and cultivating an authentic church experience that glorifies God and exceeds all expectations. Their unwavering compassion for people along with their faithfulness to build into God's people, PURPOSE, POWER, and PRAISE will continue yielding great returns for them in this time and for generations to come.

The Hilliards have committed to the parental oversight of three lovely daughters: Tina Hilliard Egans, husband Terry Egans, Irishea Hilliard Lewis, husband Jeffery Lewis, and Preashea Hilliard. The Hilliards are also very proud to have four grandchildren: Ira Emanuel, Briona Janae, Ivan Harrison, and Jonathan Sean-Michael. All the children and grandchildren have been marked for ministry with all the adult children currently working in full time ministry with their parents.

To contact Dr. Hilliard
please visit **www.newlight.org**.

Fast. Easy.
Convenient.

For the latest Harrison House product information and author news, look no further than your computer. All the details on our powerful, life-changing products are just a click away. New releases, E-mail subscriptions, testimonies, monthly specials—find it all in one place. Visit harrisonhouse.com today!

harrisonhouse

The Harrison House Vision

Proclaiming the truth and the power
Of the Gospel of Jesus Christ
With excellence;

Challenging Christians to
Live victoriously,
Grow spiritually,
Know God intimately.

Made in the USA
Middletown, DE
07 July 2021